Cambridge Elements ☰

Elements in Child Development
edited by
Marc H. Bornstein
National Institute of Child Health and Human Development, Bethesda
Institute for Fiscal Studies, London
UNICEF, New York City

GIFTEDNESS IN CHILDHOOD

Robert J. Sternberg
Cornell University

Ophélie A. Desmet
Valdosta State University

CAMBRIDGE
UNIVERSITY PRESS

Shaftesbury Road, Cambridge CB2 8EA, United Kingdom

One Liberty Plaza, 20th Floor, New York, NY 10006, USA

477 Williamstown Road, Port Melbourne, VIC 3207, Australia

314–321, 3rd Floor, Plot 3, Splendor Forum, Jasola District Centre,
New Delhi – 110025, India

103 Penang Road, #05–06/07, Visioncrest Commercial, Singapore 238467

Cambridge University Press is part of Cambridge University Press & Assessment,
a department of the University of Cambridge.

We share the University's mission to contribute to society through the pursuit of
education, learning and research at the highest international levels of excellence.

www.cambridge.org
Information on this title: www.cambridge.org/9781009475990

DOI: 10.1017/9781009310819

First published 2023

A catalogue record for this publication is available from the British Library

ISBN 978-1-009-47599-0 Hardback
ISBN 978-1-009-31083-3 Paperback
ISSN 2632-9948 (online)
ISSN 2632-993X (print)

Giftedness in Childhood

Elements in Child Development

DOI: 10.1017/9781009310819

First published online: December 2023

Robert J. Sternberg
Cornell University

Ophélie A. Desmet
Valdosta State University

Author for correspondence: Robert J. Sternberg, robert.sternberg@gmail.com

Abstract: Giftedness often is defined in a transactional way: individuals give something in return for getting something from authorities who label them as gifted; the labeling authority then expects those individuals identified as "gifted" to act in ways that justify the label. The authors place emphasis on transformational giftedness – giftedness that serves to make the world a better place. This Element stresses the importance of intelligence, not the kind of narrow intelligence measured by IQ tests and their proxies, but rather the kind of broad intelligence used to adapt to a variety of real-world environments. The authors further discuss the nature of dual exceptionality, whereby individuals may be identified as having a disability yet at the same time act in gifted ways and thereby harbor the potential to contribute to the world in some distinguished fashion.

Keywords: giftedness, transformational giftedness, transactional giftedness, adaptive intelligence, intelligence

ISBNs: 9781009475990 (HB), 9781009310833 (PB), 9781009310819 (OC)
ISSNs: 2632-9948 (online), 2632-993X (print)

Contents

1 What Is Giftedness, Anyway?

Wolfgang Amadeus Mozart was a gifted composer – one of the most gifted in history. But would he have been recognized as gifted, or even have been gifted, if his family did not provide him with abundant opportunities to engage with music and the music profession? Mozart's father, Johann Georg Leopold Mozart, was himself a composer as well as a violinist. He not only was himself distinguished but also had the connections in the musical world to introduce young Wolfgang to people who could advance Wolfgang's career. What if the very same boy had been born to a father who was a laborer, or to a father who wanted his son only to be an accountant, or in a society that forbade music?

A central theme of this Element is that giftedness is not just something one is born with. It is not something that is stored somewhere in one's brain or otherwise in one's head or body. Giftedness certainly emanates from a person, but only in interaction with the environmental context in which a person lives and with the kinds of tasks that the person encounters while developing (Sternberg, 2023a; Ziegler, 2005; Ziegler & Stoeger, 2007). Moreover, it is not just an individual phenomenon, it is also a collective one (Sternberg, 2023b).

Educators did not "discover" giftedness; largely, they invented it (Borland, 2005; Reis & Renzulli, 2009). In this Element, we view the invention of giftedness in terms of a pentagonal theory of labeling of giftedness (Sternberg, 1993; Sternberg & Zhang, 1995). This theory deals with the way people use the term "giftedness," in other words, how they come to label certain people and actions as gifted, and others as not. The pentagonal theory designates people as *gifted* if they meet all of five labeling criteria.

First, gifted people must excel in some identifiable way. They differentiate themselves from others by doing something much better than others do it.

Second, the way in which gifted people excel is relatively rare statistically. In other words, it is an excellence that relatively few people display.

Third, people labeled as "gifted" must be able in some identifiable way to demonstrate their excellence. They cannot be excellent merely in the imagination or because someone says they are. They have to show it somehow.

Fourth, people identified as gifted must be productive in demonstrating their giftedness. They need to find ways consistently to show their gift or gifts. One performance does not suffice: gifted people need to show their gifts on a repeated basis.

Fifth and finally, whatever the people identified as gifted are excellent at must be valued by persons in positions of authority in some group or groups – those who are authorized to label people as "gifted" or not.

Whenever we talk about giftedness in this Element, we are talking about someone who (1) excels identifiably, (2) is relatively rare in their excellence, (3) demonstrates the excellence, (4) does so productively, and (5) is valued by authorities in some discipline or field. We will not keep referring to these criteria, but they underlie our entire discussion.

The pentagonal theory shows that giftedness is not just "in the person" (Sternberg, 2023a). It shows the extent to which giftedness is a collective concept (Sternberg, 2023b): it is a collaboration between those individuals who perform in a certain way and those who value the way those individuals perform. In a way, it is like a musical performance: one needs a performer, of course, but one also needs an appreciative audience. If there were only one individual in the world, with no audience, there would arise no concept of "giftedness," no matter how well that one person did anything. And for musical performers to reach where they are, usually, there have been many teachers, supportive parents, colleagues, and others who helped them get there. Moreover, during that performer's life course, there are many ups and downs, successes and failures, ascensions and crashes that make them who they are. So it is with gifted individuals (Dabrowski, 1964).

Gifted individuals can be gifted in many different ways. They may be exceptional writers, musicians, dancers, soldiers, actors, scientists, or whatever. When they are young, they often are recognized simply as students. In an ideal world, those who are identified as gifted when children would, as adults, give back to the world and not just devote their resources to their self-enhancement (Sternberg, in press).

What is valued by societies changes over time. Any theory of giftedness that includes content, therefore, has a kind of life expectancy, just as people and other living beings do.

In 1925, the life expectancy for men was 57.6 years and that for women was 60.6 years (life expectancy in the United States, 1900–98). This life expectancy was actually a considerable increase from 1905, twenty years earlier, when the respective life expectancies were 47.3 years and 50.2 years. In 2023, the average man in the United States will live to 76.6 years and the average woman to 81.6 years. Unfortunately, their life spans rank only 46 worldwide. They would live longer if they came from Japan, where the average life expectancy is 81.9 years for men and 88.1 years for women (Worldometer, 2023b).

Obviously, the world has changed, at least in terms of life expectancy. Prenatal care is better, medical knowledge has increased enormously, nutrition is better, and health practices are better. For example, smoking is much less common now than it was a century ago. We know that we have to limit our intake of red meat, sugar, and saturated fats. We all can consider ourselves fortunate, at least from the standpoint of longevity, to live now rather than a century ago. As our physical health has improved, our thinking about it has changed as well. But our thinking has not changed about all matters for which a change is needed. In some areas, we are stubbornly stuck on old ideas that no longer work well.

It is perhaps odd that, whereas nutritional and medical practices have changed so much over the course of a century, aspects of psychological and educational practice have changed hardly at all. In 1925, when the life expectancy of the senior author of this Element would have been 57.6 years (he is writing at an age well beyond 57 or 58), Terman (1925) published the first results of his longitudinal study of the gifted. To this end, he used a test he had first published in 1916, which came to be called the Stanford-Binet Intelligence Scales (Terman, 1916). The current version of the same test, the fifth edition, is in active use for identifying gifted children and adults (Roid, 2003). It is perhaps not a great sign that, as this Element is being written, the current (fifth) edition of the Stanford-Binet Intelligence Scales was published twenty years ago.

To understand the field of giftedness today, one must understand how it, or any field, could have remained so nearly static over such a long period of time – essentially, a century. What kind of field does not much change over the course of a century, and what does it tell us about a field when, a century after its inception, it is still doing much the same stuff as it was doing when the average man did not reach sixty years of age? Why has our thinking gotten stuck?

2 Societal Fixation on IQ

Terman's (1925) thinking was that the main basis for identifying the gifted ought to be IQ (intelligence quotient). This is the quantity that originally was computed by dividing a person's so-called mental age – the age at which the mind operates – by their chronological age, the age they have reached physically, and multiplying the quotient by 100. Today, IQs are rarely computed in this way, but rather by percentiles, or percentages of individuals a particular person's score exceeds. In other words, your IQ today is determined not by some function of your mental age, but rather by how much better you do on the test than others of your same chronological age.

That conception of giftedness as based in IQ has lasted a long time indeed. Some would believe it has lasted so long because it is essentially correct – IQ or some derivative of it, they believe, is what matters for outstanding intellectual accomplishments (e.g., Deary, 2020; Gottfredson, 1997; Herrnstein & Murray, 1994; Kuncel et al., 2014; Lubinski & Benbow, 2006, 2020; Murray, 1998; Sackett et al., 2009, 2020; Schmidt & Hunter, 1998). Yet so many psychologists and educators have found the notion of giftedness as inhering in IQ to be inadequate and have proposed their own views, summarized in some edited books and to be explicated later in this Element (e.g., Heller et al., 2000; Pfeiffer, 2018; Sternberg & Ambrose, 2021; Sternberg et al., 2022; Sternberg & Davidson, 1986, 2005, Sternberg & Reis, 2004).

Most of those who have concerns about the use of IQ and its proxies – tests such as the SAT and ACT that have different names but that are essentially IQ tests (Frey & Detterman, 2004; Koenig et al., 2008; Sackett et al., 2020) – are not "anti-IQ" in the sense that they believe IQ tests tell us nothing or somehow provide seriously erroneous information. Rather, they believe that IQ tests provide some information about giftedness that is useful for some students in some circumstances. But they believe there is more to giftedness than just IQ, as this Element will show. As just one early example, Renzulli (1978) proposed that giftedness involves above-average (not necessarily exceptional) ability, but also creativity and task commitment (motivation). He later greatly expanded his model to include schoolwide enrichment that would provide to all students the kind of education that previously had been given primarily to gifted students (Renzulli & Reis, 1993, 1994; Renzulli et al., 2006).

Gifted programs today often use indices beyond IQ to identify students as "gifted," but the indices they use, such as the SAT, ACT, GRE, and many other tests, are rather strong correlates of IQ. Even school grades are correlates of IQ, although not as strongly as the IQ proxy tests that measure essentially the same things.

Why is IQ inadequate and why has it lasted so long as the primary measure for identifying giftedness? Why do measures of anything continue to be used long past their expiration date? For example, the body mass index is still used by many to assess health, even though the measure is severely flawed (Nordqvist, 2022). It fails to take into account such variables as muscle mass, height, age, bone density, overall body composition, and both sex and racial differences.

Table 1 shows the difference between what we call "gifted" performance versus what we call gifted performance (Sternberg, in press). "Gifted" perform-ance is the kind of performance measured by intelligence tests. Gifted perform-ance is the kind of performance one needs to excel in the real, everyday world. The table compares the kinds of skills one needs to succeed at a high level on intelligence tests with the kinds of skills needed to succeed at a high level in the world. The contrast, we suggest, is striking. On the one hand, there may be some transfer from the IQ test solving skills to the real world, as suggested by the correlation between IQ test scores and various kinds of real-world performances (Sackett et al., 2020). On the other hand, there may be some negative transfer – that is, worsening of performance as a result of the skills. Someone who is

Table 1 Why being "gifted" does not equal truly being gifted[a]

Difference	"Gifted" issue	"Gifted" individual example	Gifted issue	Gifted individual example
Type of answer	Right versus wrong	What does "exacerbate" mean?	More adaptive versus less adaptive	How can we decrease air pollution?
Structure of path to solution	Well-structured: clear, often unique path to unique solution	How many loaves of bread is 50 percent of fifty loaves?	Ill-structured: multiple fuzzy paths to partial solutions	When is 50% of a loaf of bread better than fifty loaves of bread?
Emotional/ideological resonance	Low emotional/ ideological resonance, so usually clear thinking	If five out of fifty people who are vaccinated get the disease against which they are vaccinated, what is the vaccine's efficacy?	High emotional/ ideological resonance, so often clouded thinking	You have been ordered to schedule your boss to attend an in-person meeting with other bosses. You know your boss has COVID–19. What do you do?
Life stakes	Low and thus low stakes if a solution is wrong	What are the effects of long-term doses of radioactivity on people?	Often high and thus high need for a good solution	You gave your boss an expensive necklace from a collection of jewelry that was recalled because of radioactivity. What should you do?

Table 1 (cont.)

Difference	"Gifted" issue	"Gifted" individual example	Gifted issue	Gifted individual example
Life contextualization	Decontextualized problems weakly contextualized	For what kind of illnesses is Vincristine used?	Highly contextualized problems strongly related to life events	You need medicine you cannot afford. Your sister, a nurse, offers to steal it for you. What do you say?
Need for problem recognition	None: problems are given by test	What is a pandemic and what are two great pandemics in history?	Great: one has to recognize that the problem even exists	What are the signs that a pandemic may be starting?
Need for problem definition	Low: problems are usually defined by test	During the early 1800s, what were arguments some people used to justify rebelling against the union of states in the United States?	High: problems are poorly defined	Why does slavery continue to exist in some parts of the world?
Time for solution	Low: problems can be solved in a few seconds to a few minutes	What number comes next in the following series: 2, 5, 9, 14, ?	High: problems are addressed over time but often cannot be definitively solved even then	How can we avoid polarization of political and ideological groups?

	Low		High	
Need to search for information	Low: information needed for solution given in the test problem	Bobby bought ten cherries and paid $1.50. How much did each cherry cost?	High: Information needed for solution has to be located on Internet or elsewhere	How would someone figure out the cost to society of each case of COVID–19?
Need to evaluate information	Information given in test problem is generally viewed as credible and consistent	Abraham Lincoln is often viewed as the best president in US history. Why?	Information sources are often low in credibility and mutually contradictory	Abraham Lincoln is often viewed as the best president in US history. Why?
Need to work groups	Problems are solved individually without consultation being allowed	Figure out how to compute the area of a hexagon. You must work individually without consulting anyone else	Problems are solved individually or in groups but with consultation of others, including experts	Working as a group, figure out how to compute the area of house that needs carpeting
Relevance of ethical thinking and action	Ethics are not important for solution	What are the stages in Kohlberg's theory of moral development?	Ethics often are important for solution	If your wife were desperately ill and the only hope of cure was to smuggle unapproved medication that could not be legally imported into the country, would you do it?

a Based in part on Sternberg, R. J. (in press). In the movies, someone always defuses the time bomb – in real life, not so much: what is wrong with contemporary conceptions of giftedness. In C. Fischer, C. Fischer-Ontrup, F. Käpnick, N. Neuber, & C. (Eds.), *Potenziale erkennen – Talente entwickeln – Bildung nachhaltig gestalten.* Waxmann.

skilled in solving clean, neat, abstract IQ test problems with no rough edges may try to solve real-world problems in the same way that they try to solve IQ test problems, with bad or even disastrous results.

There are many reasons why the traditional approach to giftedness remains, even when it is, at best, incomplete, and at worst, counterproductive.

1. **Entrenchment.** The field has been doing, more or less, the same thing for a century – identifying the gifted by IQ and related measures and then teaching in ways that emphasize academic acceleration or enrichment. It is difficult to change practices that are entrenched and that have become standard practice over a long period of time.

2. **Training.** Teachers of the gifted and those who train them have been inculcated with a certain model. It is what they understand and know how to use. Changing identification and labeling practices would involve a great deal of training, up and down the line from training teachers of the gifted to preparing administrators for changes, and resources for gifted programs are hard enough to find without adding to the problems they currently have in getting funded.

3. **Benefits to Those Who Already Are Benefited.** There is an expression that "history is written by victors." The expression is attributed to Winston Churchill, but it is not clear who was the first truly to say it. But those who are in positions of power, in education or any other field, are the winners of a societal race. They were identified as standing out, often by the very measures that now are being questioned. Yet, a fundamental principle of interpersonal attraction is that we are attracted to people like ourselves (Sternberg, 1998b). We choose as gifted those who fit a societal prototype of success, which resembles those in power who get to choose, largely, what the prototype is. These tests create what sometimes is viewed as a meritocracy trap (Markovits, 2020; Sandel, 2021). Society comes to believe in them and in their value as establishing a "true" meritocracy. They then become self-perpetuating as those who have been benefited by the tests assume positions of power and look for others like themselves.

4. **Superstition.** Few adults believe they have superstitions. That is because they (mistakenly) call them by another name: "facts." As has been pointed out elsewhere (Sternberg, 2022a), when a society identifies what it believes to be a marker of future success, that belief results in a self-fulfilling prophecy so that the identified marker does indeed become a predictor of future success. So, for example, if employers believe that going to a particular set of universities is a marker of future success, they are more likely to hire people from those universities, thereby opening a path to future success denied to those going to universities outside that set. Those who did

not go to the chosen universities might have done as well or better at the jobs – they simply never got the chance to show what they could do. The same would apply to preferences for a particular sex, ethnic, racial, socioeconomic, or other group.

5. **Prediction of School Success.** Intelligence quotient tests and their proxies predict school success, which is what teachers observe on a day-to-day basis. It is generally easier to teach high-IQ students and they require less intervention on the part of teachers, at least for them to show satisfactory performance in school. Intelligence quotient tests also predict later successes of various kinds of societally sanctioned accomplishments, such as four-year graduation from college, prestige of college, income, and even longevity (Herrnstein & Murray, 1994). So, what's not to like if one relies on predictive power as an index of the value of an assessment?

There are many problems with IQ testing, such as sometimes questionable differences in scores among different ethnic, racial, and other groups. But the greatest problem is an obvious one. The people who contribute the most to society – who are truly gifted in what they have to give – cannot be detected by IQ tests. Does anyone know or care what the IQs are of great authors, artists, composers, journalists, engineers, politicians? Indeed, too many politicians who have the IQs to get themselves into prestigious colleges and universities seem not even to think rationally.

This Element argues for a conception of giftedness very different from the prevailing one. But to understand the new conception we present and why we believe in it, you need to understand the old conception and why it has endured for a century. How could that happen? Why do people put up with it? Would they put up with century-old medical tests or interventions or nutritional advice? Would they listen, with a straight face, to doctors in advertisements telling them which cigarette to smoke? How could a field lie fallow for a century and, somehow, not many people notice? Have psychology and education gone nowhere in 100 years? Actually, they have gone pretty far. The psychology of today looks little like the psychology of a century ago. It was just about a century ago that Watson (1930) said:

> "Give me a dozen healthy infants, well-formed, and my own specified world to bring them up in, and I'll guarantee to take any one – at random and train him to become any type of specialist I might select: doctor, lawyer, artist, merchant-chief and, yes, even beggar-man and thief, regardless of his talents, penchants, tendencies, abilities, vocations and race of his ancestors."

If we are way past that – who really believes that anymore – why are we still with what Lewis Terman told us even earlier?

3 A Strange Early History of the Field of Giftedness and Some Modern Notions

Terman was a professor at Stanford University, then, as now, a prestigious institution of higher learning. Terman was perhaps the first American psychologist to take a serious interest in the gifted – who they were, how they could be identified, and how they could be developed (Terman, 1925). Terman took a test developed by Alfred Binet and Theodore Simon (1905) in early twentieth-century France, had it translated into English, revised it, and then used it to identify who among his sample in California was gifted and who was not. Terman largely identified giftedness with level of IQ, selecting only those in a small fraction of 1 percent of the population (generally, IQs over 140) as gifted.

What did Terman (1925) find in his study? His findings, and those of his successors who took over the longitudinal study of giftedness (e.g., Sears, 1977), were enough to fill many volumes. But several are especially noteworthy because they help us understand the field of giftedness.

First, the large majority of the children Terman identified as gifted were White and middle- to upper-middle class. Terman was what today would be called an "elitist," and he also believed in racial differences in intelligence. He was an ardent hereditarian and a supporter of eugenics. So, the fact that the test he used identified mostly the "usual suspects" was not a problem for him; on the contrary, it confirmed what he already believed.

Second, the data disconfirmed some negative stereotypes about individuals who are intellectually gifted – that they are, for the most part, physically challenged, social misfits, and generally disagreeable people. These were powerful stereotypes, and ones that Terman did society a favor by disconfirming.

Third, participants in the study performed far better than would have been expected, on average, in a variety of measures of societal success. Within the elite IQs of the group, IQ mattered but not so much for societal success in terms of prestige of job, salary, awards, and the like. Many other variables came into play. Individuals differed greatly in personality, motivation, and the opportunities they sought out, and far more than IQ made a difference in traditional measures of societal success. But their superior IQs were certainly associated with greater success in traditional measures of societal success.

This last finding was a powerful propellant for IQ testing and the later administration of various kinds of proxy IQ tests. If the tests predict varied measures of success – education level, professional accomplishments, good health, marital success, enhanced income, and other measures of desirable outcomes (see, for example, Gottfredson, 1997; Herrnstein & Murray, 1994; Schmidt & Hunter, 1998) – they must have something, and presumably, a lot going for them. In particular, if they predict who will perform in a gifted way later in life, isn't that prima facie evidence for their validity?

"Correlation does not imply causation." This means that the fact that two variables are correlated does not imply that either causes the other. For example, height is associated with mental abilities over the course of the life span, but not because being taller leads people to be smarter. Rather, as people grow older, they grow taller, but also as they grow older, their mental powers increase as their brains develop and they become more educated. Height is an irrelevant variable that just happens to be associated with something else – namely, education and brain development. To consider a slightly more subtle example, for much of US history, there was a strong correlation between being a White male and being financially successful. One might have concluded that White males have some inherent characteristic that leads them to be successful – maybe more intelligence or charm or leadership skill. The explanation stemmed not from any characteristic inherent to White males, but rather from societal stereotypes: only White males were given the opportunities in education and jobs to attain the highest levels of success. In another society, one that preferred some other set of characteristics, those other characteristics, such as being of a particular religion, would lead to success because only people of the approved religion were (or are) allowed into the highest paying and most prestigious jobs.

The kind of logic that undermines the connection between correlations and success is very relevant, as it turns out, to the issue of the success of IQ tests and their proxies – tests with other names that nevertheless function like IQ tests. Suppose that a society did indeed believe that height is an important precursor of societal success – that tall people are more gifted than short ones. Such a view is not too far off from societal views, as tall people do tend to be more successful societally (Dittmann, 2004). Now, because people in our hypothetical society believe in height as a measure of potential for future success, they use height as a predictor of who will succeed and who will fail. To be admitted to gifted programs in K-12, one must be taller; to be admitted to more prestigious colleges and universities, one must be taller; and to be hired for the most responsible positions, one must be taller. This system lasts over a number of years. Then, inevitably, some well-meaning psychologists study predictors of adult success. They discover that height is highly associated with success, and they publish their highly statistically significant results. Apparently, height does matter for success. The system is a great success! Tall people are succeeding in droves, while short people are failing. Thus, an erroneous conclusion is reached.

Of course, the same results could have been obtained through religious preferences (only people of the approved religion are given better opportunities), sex (only people of one sex – probably males – are given better opportunities), skin color (only people of a particular skin color – probably white – are given better opportunities), parental wealth (only people with rich parents are given better opportunities), or really, anything else. If one designs society to favor certain groups, those groups will, on average, do better, sometimes far better, because they were favored every step of the way. But here's the important thing: the favored people are unlikely to attribute their success to contrived, indeed, rigged societal engineering. Rather, they will see their success as fairly and dutifully earned. They will not only believe; they will believe they *know* that they have been successful because they are, well, better than others. And they will want to ensure their own children enjoy the same benefits they have enjoyed. And they will want to ensure that society is fair to others who are meritorious like them – and who happen to share the same societal preference mechanisms.

The advantage of doing well on whatever criterion or criteria society sets to be taken seriously is much greater than any one single decision, such as admission to a gifted program, a prestigious private K-12 school, or a college. The advantages are diffused into so many places that they become uncountable. Admission to an elite college or university, for example, guarantees nothing. What it does is that it opens doors. For example, students are more likely to be taught by the movers and shakers in the field. They, in turn, have the connections to other universities and other institutions that can help move their career forward. One of us has experienced this kind of connection personally: his undergraduate advisor at Yale was a good friend of his future graduate advisor at Stanford. Connections matter (Zuckerman, 1983). Moreover, the other students one meets in more prestigious institutions are themselves likely to be among the movers and shakers of the next generation and getting to know them paves the way for success. It is not only in universities, of course. Getting jobs in more prestigious businesses or nonprofits paves the way for jobs in other prestigious businesses or nonprofits.

Then there is the way society treats you. Society does not treat everyone equally of course. It prefers those who, by some measure, show they should be preferred. Students who are labeled as gifted will have opportunities in their school careers and later on that other students only can dream of. Put simply, identification as "special" almost without regard to how one is special sets up a self-fulfilling prophecy whereby one is treated as special and, as a result, may very well become special.

We have proposed that the conventional conception of intelligence is inadequate – that it accounts for part of intelligence and of the intelligence that contributes to giftedness, but not for all of what matters (Sternberg, 2021a). We believe the current conception of intelligence is woefully inadequate to the demands of the twenty-first century and that it is not only holding us back, but actually is making things much worse than they need to be, such as pollution, global climate change, severe income disparities, and proliferation of nuclear weapons, to name a few. It preserves an order of "gifted" people, some and perhaps many of whom are not up to the tasks facing the world today, any more than were the royalty or the scions of wealthy families of the past (or present).

Consider some of the serious problems facing the world today.

Certainly, one such problem is global climate change. Parts of the world, especially small islands and low-lying coastal areas, are becoming uninhabitable because they are being inundated with water. In the Mississippi Delta and coastal Louisiana, a football field's worth of land disappears roughly every 100 minutes (Kolbert, 2019). Since the 1930s, Louisiana has lost in excess of 2,000 square miles of land mass (Land Loss, 2023). When one of us was young, he grew up with a romantic notion of the Pacific Islands, perhaps as a result of a musical he attended, *South Pacific,* by Richard Rodgers and Oscar Hammerstein. But today, at least five of the Pacific Islands have vanished underwater, and others are threatened as well (GVI, 2022).

Consider a second problem, air pollution. World Health Organization (WHO) statistics show that almost the entire population of the world – 99 percent to be more nearly precise – breathe air that has levels of pollutants that exceed WHO standards, leading to seven million premature deaths per year (World Health Organization, 2023a). Large numbers become abstractions. Looked at another way, if one were to count each of these deaths, one per second, it would take 11 days, 13 hours, 46 minutes, and 40 seconds to count from 1 to 1,000,000, counting full time with no breaks for eating, sleeping, or going to the bathroom.

Consider, third, water pollution. Water pollution kills more people annually than does war and all other forms of violence of humans against humans combined (Denchak, 2023). Agricultural pollution is the chief source of contaminants flowing into rivers and streams. Sewage, wastewater, and industrial pollution contribute as well. In the year 2015, according to Denchak, water pollution is estimated to have caused 1.8 million deaths and sickened in excess of 1 billion people. You, the reader, may well have been one of the latter, whether you knew it or not. The oceans are now filled with waste. For example, it is estimated that there are now at least 5.25 trillion pieces of plastic of varying sizes in our oceans. That amounts to 46,000 pieces for every square mile of the oceans. Together, they weigh as much as 269,000 tons (Condor Ferries, 2023). Those pieces of plastic are ingested by fish and then by the animals that eat fish, meaning that if you eat fish, you are eating the plastic which fish have ingested.

In 2022, more than 6,000 children and teenagers were either injured or killed by gun violence (Hauck, 2023). Less than one hour had passed at the beginning of 2022 before the first killing. As of March 27, 2023, there already had been thirteen school shootings in the United States (Education Week, 2023). On the day we write these words (April 10, 2023), there have been more mass shootings in the world than there have been days in the year (Alfonseca, 2023). The response to all this? Platitudes, and little else.

One might wonder why we are including this very small sample of the problems the world faces today in a book about the gifted. The reason is that these are the kinds of problems the world of the present faces and the world of the future will face. The main problems the world faces are not ones that resemble the rarefied, artificial, and really, beside-the-point kinds of problems that appear on standardized tests and in much of the material schools require students to learn. Knowing how to compute the areas of various irregular figures, for example, may be useful to future engineers and architects, but all of this assumes that there will be a world left that is inhabited by humans for which there are humans to fill jobs.

Intelligence quotient may be useful for various things, but for solving the problems of the world, it has not proven itself to be very useful. Flynn (1987, 2012, 2016, 2020) found that average IQs rose 30 points during the twentieth century around the world. This was a stunning increase. It means that the number of score points on an IQ test that would have yielded a score of 130 in 1900 would have yielded a score of about 100 in 2000. In other words, the individual who was identified as gifted in IQ in 1900 would have been identified as merely average in 2000. There is now some evidence that, in the twenty-first century, the world is experiencing a reverse Flynn effect (e.g., Bratsberg & Rogeberg, 2018; Pietschnig & Gittler, 2015; Teasdale & Owen, 2005). But the losses are nowhere as large as the gains of the preceding century.

Within days of a massive school shooting in Nashville, Tennessee (March 28, 2023), the Governor of Florida, a graduate of Yale University, a prestigious Ivy League University that prides itself on admitting only very intellectually able students, signed a bill sponsored by the state Republican Party allowing people to carry concealed firearms anywhere in the State of Florida without a permit (Bushard, 2023). The bill was approved with over-whelming support by the Florida State Legislature. Florida thereby became the twenty-sixth state in the United States to allow such carrying of weapons without a permit.

DeSantis, at the time of signing the bill, was a presidential candidate who perhaps was willing to do whatever it would take to become the presidential candidate of his political party. He also had taken on Disney over their support of gay rights (Atterbury, 2022). But his support of enhanced gun rights is widely supported by his political party. The laws in the United States put the country at odds with the rest of the so-called developed world, and actually, most of the rest of the world too (Leach-Kemon & Sirull, 2022).

Whatever it is that IQ buys us – and it does correlate with a long list of societally sanctioned criteria (Sackett et al., 2020) – it does not seem to have been particularly effective in solving world problems. As we write on April 4, 2023, Russia, a perpetrator of twenty-first-century genocide (Hook, 2022), is president of the UN Security Council. It does not take a high IQ to fathom the absurdity of that situation. How would we look back on the powerful people alive during World War II if they made Adolf Hitler president of any roughly comparable world body (the UN did not exist yet during World War II)?

4 Giftedness Is Not a Property of Person

To recapitulate, the most basic assumption of gifted education appears to be that giftedness is a property of a person – that it is something that is somehow inside some people and not others. Those who have "giftedness" thus are identified by existing tests or other measures, and those who do not have "giftedness" are not so identified.

This view is problematic and wrong. At some level, we all know this. We know people who did well in school or who had sky-high standardized test scores who cannot get anything in their life to work out right. Almost all of us know others who did not test well and yet seem to have achieved goals that we could only dream of. Another way to look at this kind of situation is to think in terms of what it means to be gifted (or talented) in different milieus.

A gifted violinist can play by memory, nearly flawlessly and with astonishing musical virtuosity, the Beethoven Violin Concerto in D, keeping in time with the accompanying orchestra and complementing them in tone and volume.

A gifted (but sleazy) politician can get people to vote for them even when they are in politics only for their personal gain and care only about accumulating power, money, and other resources.

A gifted statesperson (in contrast) working at a national level can negotiate with representatives of foreign powers that have opposing interests and nevertheless strike an agreement that benefits both countries.

Of course, a list such as this could be as long as this Element. But how many of the accomplishments on this list can be captured by an IQ test, or really, any other test or even set of tests? Clearly, many of these accomplishments depend on one's being educated in a certain field. Despite the importance of deliberate practice to becoming an expert (Ericsson & Pool, 2017), probably none of us is on the way to becoming the next Albert Einstein, Wolfgang Amadeus Mozart,

Pablo Picasso, William Shakespeare, or LeBron James, no matter how much we work on developing our gifts and talents.

The terms "gifts" and "talents" are used in different ways by different scholars (see Sternberg & Ambrose, 2021). Some scholars use the term "gifts" to refer to potentials and "talents" to refer to "developed gifts." Others use the term gifts, in a related way, as heritable, whereas talents are developed environmentally. Sometimes "gifts" is a more general term, referring to general abilities and "talents" to accomplishments or the potential for accomplishments in specific domains. Here, however, these differences are not relevant, because both gifts and talents, however defined, are not viewed as properties of individuals.

Giftedness is not a property of an individual, but rather of an interaction among an individual, a task or set of tasks, and a situation or set of situations (Sternberg, 2021b, 2023b; Sternberg et al., 2022; Sternberg & Preiss, 2022; Tromp & Sternberg, 2022). The individual who is gifted in a society that values IQ testing may or may not be gifted in a society that values hunting and gathering or one that values political subservience. In a dictatorship – of which there are many in the world today – having a high IQ will buy you nothing but a prison term or worse, if you are not subservient to the government, no matter how bad it is. One could say that those who land in prison are IQ-gifted, but they may not be able to exploit their gifts if they are locked away, especially in solitary confinement, or if they are pushed out of a high window in a homicide – as has happened with frightening frequency in Russia – made to look like a suicide.

The tasks matter. Intelligence quotient test scores may be valued in US society and in other societies, but their value really depends on the life a person lives. The skills that make one stand out as a leader in a democracy may kill one in a dictatorship. The skills that make one a leader in a dictatorship may lead to one being viewed as an obedient, mediocre "yes-man" in a democracy. The skills that lead one to be able to feed one's family in a hunting-and-gathering society may be worth little in an advanced techno-logical society, but the reverse is true as well. Moreover, in societies where one's choice of occupation is severely constrained – for example, one may be gifted to do a job but a member of a caste, a religion, a perceived nationality, or a socially defined race or ethnicity that is held back – all the gifts one has may amount to little. For example, in societies that are explicitly caste-based, as in India (Sternberg & Grigorenko, 1999), some people simply are not given the opportunities others are handed on a silver platter. The children of the rich, almost anywhere, are bestowed with advantages that are not available to the children of the poor.

The context in which one lives has an enormous effect on what is "gifted." Children who do not do well in school might have hidden talents that just do not show up in the context of the school (Ellis et al., 2020, 2023). Consider, for example, rural Kenya, where we have conducted some cultural research. We were interested in rural Kenyan conceptions of the nature of intelligence (Grigorenko et al., 2001). The rural Kenyan people we studied had four different terms in their conception of intelligence – *rieko* (which included knowledge, including academic knowledge and skills), *luoro* (respect and deference), *winjo* (understanding of how to deal with everyday real-life problems), and *paro* (initiative and drive). Only the first term, "rieko," related clearly to the kind of academic performance schools value. Someone could be gifted in rieko but not be gifted in the other aspects of intelligence, or they could be gifted in another aspect but not rieko. Academic skills simply did not have the priority in rural Kenya that they have in some contemporary Western countries.

We conducted a research study in Usenge, Kenya, which is near Kisumu, a large city in Kenya. Who is gifted depends on environmental context. We studied the abilities of school-age children to adapt to their indigenous everyday environment. We wished to create a test of intelligence in the context of real adaptation to the environment (Sternberg et al., 2001). The test we created measured children's informal and usually tacit knowledge regarding an important aspect of adaptation – natural herbal medicines that the villagers believed could be used to combat parasitic illnesses, and that indeed had been shown to be successful. For these children, combating malaria, schistosomiasis, hookworm, whipworm, and other parasitic illnesses was a top adaptive priority, because these diseases were prevalent and could be extremely debilitating, resulting in loss of time in school, impaired cognitive development, and restricted social lives. More than 95 percent of the children we studied suffered from parasitic illnesses at one time or another.

Much of intelligence in any culture depends on tacit knowledge, or what one needs to know to adapt to and succeed in an environment. Tacit knowledge is typically not taught explicitly in school or elsewhere. Usually, it is not even verbalized out loud (Sternberg et al., 2000). It is something one picks up from life experience.

On average, children in the rural Kenyan villages in which we worked used their tacit knowledge of these natural herbal medicines one time per week. They used the knowledge both to medicate themselves and to medicate others. These tests thus measured intelligence as adaptive to real environments, not as imagined authors of rarefied intelligence tests.

Three lessons from this research are worth noting before continuing.

First, the mental processes underlying intelligence in rural Kenya or anywhere else are not all that different or perhaps even different at all as a function of culture (Sternberg, 2020a, 2020b). What differs is how the processes play out contextually. In any environment, to be gifted or even to function at high levels, one needs to be able to deploy certain executive mental processes, which, since 1985, Sternberg has called metacomponents. A high level of metacomponential functioning is important in many forms of giftedness, and may even be necessary.

Recognizing the existence of a problem. In school and on IQ tests, either a test or a teacher presents problems for children to solve. In real life, however, problems typically are not "presented." No one even says that a problem exists. One has to figure it out. For example, one of the senior author's child was bullied for a while before recognizing that something was wrong and that they had a problem. Often, in relationships, whether between children or adults, by the time one even recognizes one has a problem, it is late in the game and perhaps even too late to do anything about it. Gifted children can recognize the existence of problems before others do, if they are taught by adults to look for problems where they exist.

Defining the nature of the problem. In life, one not only has to recognize that one has a problem, one also has to figure out exactly what the problem is. Sometimes, the greatest challenge is that one knows one has a problem, but one is not sure what the problem is. Sometimes, we all feel anxiety – something is wrong – but we are not sure why. In the case of the senior author's child, the child not only had to figure out that something was wrong but also that they were being bullied. In a similar manner, the Kenyan children had to recognize that they were, or someone else was, ill, and then figure out what the illness was. Gifted children, properly educated, can produce more accurate depictions of problems, often more quickly, than can those without comparable gifts.

Deciding on the resources to allocate to the problem. Many of us, from childhood through adulthood, find ourselves busy, often with too much to do. When we have a problem that we hope to solve, we have to decide how much time, how much money, how much effort, how many resources in general we can throw at the problem. For example, the child had to figure out how big a deal to make of the bullying – let it go? talk to a parent (as happened)? talk to a teacher? talk to the bully? What? A challenge is deciding how much of a problem a problem really is.

Representing the problem and setting up a strategy for solving the problem. Exactly how is one going to solve the problem? If the child is going to talk to the bully – or a parent or a teacher – what should they say? What should they do? How do they move forward to solve the problem? Gifted children can better represent and strategize for solving problems if they are properly educated to do so.

Monitoring problem-solving while it is ongoing. How well is the problem-solving going? Is it working? If not, why not? What could be done better, if anything? Is whatever strategy the child takes to confront the bullying seemingly paying off? Gifted children have more resources to bring to bear upon monitoring, but whether they deploy them effectively is a choice they have to make.

Evaluating the problem-solving after it is done. Did the strategy work? If so, great. If not, why not? What could be done better next time? Is the situation remediable? If the bullying is ongoing, what is the next step in trying to deal with it? Gifted children can evaluate problem solutions particularly deeply, but only if they realize that their gifts do not prevent them from making mistakes, sometimes serious ones, in solving the problems.

The second lesson is that, although we have conceived of so-called general intelligence as excellence in the metacomponents described earlier in this section, the skill with which they are used varies across tasks and situations. For example, the individual who uses them effectively in playing football may not use them effectively in solving mathematics problems; the individual who uses them effectively in low-stress situations may not use them effectively in high-stress situations, or the reverse. Children and adults alike are not gifted merely by virtue of excelling in these processes, but by virtue of how they excel in them for particular tasks or classes of tasks in particular situations or classes of situations.

The third lesson to keep in mind, something of an entirely different order, is that history tends to repeat itself, in part because people learn so little from it (Santayana, 1905/1998). The problems of rural Kenyan children fighting parasitic illnesses might seem to require skills called for only in the developing world. Or they might seem passé, relevant primarily to the Middle Ages, when people fought off one plague after another. And yet, the world of the twenty-first century has faced its own version of the Plague, with close to seven million people having died of COVID-19 as of April 2023 (Worldometer, 2023a). About forty million people have died of AIDS (World Health Organization, 2023b). Many of these deaths were preventable. Are the problems faced by rural Kenyan children so different from the problems the so-called developed world faces today? And how many people, including ones of high IQ, have died because they did not learn the skills that rural Kenyan children learned to deal with the illnesses they have faced?

Here is an example of a problem the senior author's colleagues and he used in the study of intelligence in rural Kenya (note that correct answers have an asterisk next to them) (Sternberg et al., 2001):

- "A small child in your family has homa. She has a sore throat, headache, and fever. She has been sick for 3 days. Which of the following five Yadh nyaluo (Luo herbal medicines) can treat homa?
  - i. Chamama. Take the leaf and fito (sniff medicine up the nose to sneeze out illness).*
  - ii. Kaladali. Take the leaves, drink, and fito.*
  - iii. Obuo. Take the leaves and fito.*
  - iv. Ogaka. Take the roots, pound, and drink.
  - v. Ahundo. Take the leaves and fito."

Obviously, very few people in the developed world could correctly answer this or any of the other problems on the test. The rural Kenyan children did quite well. More generally, residents of the so-called developed world might be challenged to survive, and certainly to thrive, in the kinds of contexts in which these children live. Many city dwellers of the middle and upper-middle classes would be challenged to survive even in the inner-city neighborhoods that may exist nearby or, in some countries, adjacent to their homes. As in the novel *The City & The City* (Miéville, 2010), it is as though two cities coexist with each other, occupying overlapping spaces, and yet the residents of the two cities hardly recognize or deal with each other – in this case, especially the individuals in the ghetto dealing with the people from outside it. Similarly, the children who live in an urban ghetto who need to figure out how to get to and from school safely probably would not need to know how to use natural herbal medicines to combat parasitic illnesses that thrive in rural settings, especially near lakes such as Lake Victoria (Victoria Nyanza) in Uganda, Tanzania, and on the border of Kenya.

In our test, we assessed the rural Kenyan children's ability to identify the medicines, where they come from, what they are used for, and how they are dosed. We also measured fluid or abstract-reasoning-based skills and administered a test of crystallized or formal-knowledge-based skills. We gave them a vocabulary test in their indigenous language (Dholuo).

We expected little or no correlation between our test of knowledge of herbal medicines and the tests of intelligence as traditionally defined. But we were wrong: all the correlations between our test of adaptive intelligence in the rural Kenyan setting and the tests of intelligence were *negative*. In other words, the better the children did on our tests, the worse they did on the traditional Western intelligence tests. Howard Gardner (2011) as well has pointed out that different kinds of what he calls "intelligences" may show minimal correlations with each other. In our case, the correlation was negative.

Why might the relation between our adaptive-intelligence test and conventional IQ tests be negative (Prince & Geissler, 2001)? Although we cannot be sure, a plausible explanation takes into account the expectations of families and the village as a whole for their children. Many children drop out of conventional schooling before they graduate or even get close to graduation. The reason is that, in their cultural context, academic schooling can be a dead end (Sternberg & Grigorenko, 2006). There are not a lot of jobs, at least locally, for young people who are highly academically educated. Rather, jobs exist for those who have been apprenticed and learned a trade, such as to be a fisherman or a farmer. The ones who are considered "bright" in terms of local standards, therefore, are most advantaged if they drop out of formal school and take an apprenticeship. They then learn a trade that will earn them a living. So, a lot of schooling is associated with time that could have been spent in more productive and relevant pursuits.

This view may sound limited to a not-yet-industrialized culture, but it is not. The senior author has a son who was a student at one of the most prestigious business schools in the country. As a student, he was offered a large investment in a company he started, but only if he dropped out of school. The venture capital firm was not interested in funding someone who would not be working full time on the business they funded. His son dropped out. He was worried. He shouldn't have been. Today the son is CEO of a large elder healthcare company. He has done extremely well, at least by conventional societal standards as well as by his own standards of giving back to society. The logic of the venture capital firm was surprisingly similar to that in rural Kenya. You learn adaptive intelligence by doing it, not by studying for academic tests.

Usually, tests of practical and adaptive intelligence correlate close to zero with conventional academic intelligence tests (Hedlund, 2020). What we see here is that a whole literature showing positive correlations across tests, dating back to the very beginning of the twentieth century (Spearman, 1904, 1927), is conditioned on some pretty narrow assumptions – namely, that one uses the kinds of academic problems that appear on IQ tests, that they are administered under standardized testing conditions, and that they are given to people who understand the point of them, rather than just writing them off as a waste of their time.

Whereas many people in industrialized and postindustrialized societies view formal education as a positive and valuable use of time, not everyone does. On the one hand, such education raises IQ test scores, not just academic achievement (Ceci, 1996; Ritchie & Tucker-Drob, 2018). On the other hand, IQ tests are largely measures of academic and related kinds of achievement (Sternberg & Grigorenko, 2003). They were created by Binet and Simon (1916) to sort students in terms of their abilities for academic achievement. It might sound as though we, as authors, are speaking with some kind of anti-IQ bias, but no: even developers of intelligence tests often recognize that the tasks on such tests "*measure what the individual has learned*" (Kaufman, 1979, p. 11, italics in original). It is not surprising, therefore, that IQ tests predict school achievement. And at least in contemporary societies, many of these skills are relevant for adaptation to job requirements as well (Gottfredson, 1997; Schmidt & Hunter, 1998).

The results we obtained in Kenya have been found elsewhere. Parents in rural Zanzibar, as in Kenya, often keep at home the children they perceive to be the brightest. Those are the children who can be most useful for domestic tasks at home and agricultural tasks in the fields (The Economist, 2002). Moreover, street children living in Brazil often perform poorly on tests of mathematical knowledge and skills where problems are presented in terms of academic tasks. However, they perform much better when the tasks are framed in terms of the computations needed for success in their street businesses (Ceci & Roazzi, 1994; Nuñes, 1994).

In a germane series of studies, Lave (1988) found that supermarket shoppers in Berkeley, California, were generally able to perform computations that allowed them to calculate the lowest price on a supermarket product; but they often were unable to do essentially the same computations if the problems were presented in classroom settings. And even today in the United States, young people are being paid by some Silicon Valley entrepreneurs, in particular, Peter Thiel, *not* to attend college (e.g., Wieder, 2011).

What one can conclude from all this is that what is "gifted" depends very heavily on the environmental context in which a child (or adult) lives and the adaptive demands that context makes on the individual. Simply assuming that the context of the middle- to upper-middle class in the United States or anywhere else is relevant to people elsewhere is a great stretch. The skills that are valued in one place or at one time may be valued, indifferent, or actually devalued in another place or at another time. Being a shaman will not get you far in most of the United States, but it may get you very far elsewhere. Being a Catholic priest in a country that is entirely or almost entirely Muslim also may present challenges. Giftedness is not just a thing that somehow resides in a person's head. It is always in the interaction among the person, the environmental context in which that person lives, and the kinds of tasks that the environmental context presents. Even within a small community, then, giftedness may be different things for different young people, depending on how they live and where they hope to go with their lives.

5 An Alternative View of Intelligence and Giftedness

Solving number series and remembering vocabulary words are not tantamount to solving world problems. Some other conception of intelligence is needed. Toward that end, one of us has proposed the notion of *adaptive intelligence,* which is the intelligence one needs to make a positive, meaningful, and potentially enduring difference to the world, at some level (Sternberg, 2019a, 2021b). Gifted individuals thus must have a sense of what is meaningful to the world and of what is meaningful to themselves (Rodríguez-Fernández & Sternberg, 2023). On this view, intelligence is not merely about a score on a test or one's ability to solve any abstract problems that are IQ-test-like. Rather, it is about how one's intelligence, and in the case of the gifted, giftedness is deployed (Sternberg, 2021d). If one looks at truly gifted behavior, whether in young people such as Malala Yousafzai and Greta Thunberg, or in older people such as Nelson Mandela or Martin Luther King, the basis for giftedness does not appear to be merely in their IQs. What are the intellectual skills that distinguish those who display gifted behavior?

Intelligence is broader than just the analytical skills measured by IQ tests and their proxies. Adaptive intelligence – the kind used to adapt to real-world environments – involves other skills as well. One needs creative skills as well as attitudes to generate novel and useful ideas. One needs analytical skills and attitudes, as measured by conventional tests, to discern whether the ideas are good ones. One needs practical skills and attitudes to put the ideas into practice and convince others of their value. And one needs wisdom-based skills and attitudes to ensure that the ideas help to achieve some kind of common good – and to enact care and concern for others beyond oneself (Chowkase & Watve, 2021; Chowkase, 2022).

Attitudes are important, not just skills, because often people possess the skills but are not interested in using them, or use them for maladaptive purposes (Sternberg, 2022b, 2022c). Attitudes are what activate the skills and, hopefully, activate them to serve a positive purpose. How many people are intelligent, in a test-like sense, but then choose not to apply their intelligence to the problems they encounter in their lives? Their intelligence remains inert.

A common objection to expanded views of intelligence and giftedness is that the ideas may be interesting, but that intelligence and giftedness, when defined broadly, cannot be measured in a reliable and valid way. This is not the case, however. In a large study called the Rainbow Project (Sternberg & the Rainbow Project Collaborators, 2006), tests of analytical, creative, and practical thinking were given to high school and college students across the United States. The Rainbow tests more than doubled prediction of freshman year grades across a wide range of colleges and universities and greatly decreased ethnic and racial differences across groups. When one of us became Dean of Arts and Sciences at Tufts University, he and his colleagues followed up this research project with an action research project in which we used tests of analytical, creative, practical, and wise thinking for actual freshman-year admissions. That is, the results were used to make decisions about who was gifted enough to enter Tufts University, a highly selective university in the Northeast of the United States. Employing the tests greatly enhanced admissions, enabling Tufts to admit students who would otherwise not have been admitted but who had great success as students (Sternberg, 2009, 2010; Sternberg et al., 2012). The tests used at Tufts, called Kaleidoscope, also largely removed ethnic and racial group differences that had been a problem with previous tests.

The tests described here are tests that measure achievement, but also that have at times been called "ability" or "aptitude" tests. In a separate series of studies, we sought to examine whether it was possible to augment College Board Advanced Placement tests, which are advanced achievement tests, by introducing creative and practical test items. We found that introducing the new items reduced racial and ethnic group differences (Stemler et al., 2006, 2009).

We have claimed that analytical, creative, practical, and wisdom-based skills and attitudes can be measured. What exactly are they?

5.1 Analytical Skills and Attitudes

Early in the senior author's career, he believed that the problem with IQ tests was that they told score interpreters nothing about the mental processes involved in solving IQ test problems. At the time, tests such as the SAT made fairly heavy use of verbal analogy items. The *Miller Analogies Test* is composed exclusively of verbal analogies. But the problems are problematic. For example, in a verbal analogy such as assuage : ameliorate :: mitigate : ?, the correct solution does not depend on verbal reasoning so much as on sheer vocabulary knowledge. Similarly, a correct solution to the problem, watt : ohm :: power : _?___, measures information about the world, specifically about electricity, but it does not truly measure verbal reasoning.

The senior author was concerned that gifted students could be unidentified because, although they processed information well, they did not have the vocabulary and general information one needed to do well, not only on verbal analogy tests but also on other tests requiring specific academic or culturally based information. He therefore proposed an alternative theory of giftedness (Sternberg, 1981). This theory of giftedness was based on a more general theory of intelligence (Sternberg, 1977), a so-called componential theory.

The basic idea was that intelligence, in general, and giftedness in particular, should be understood not merely in terms of IQ scores, or scores on proxy tests, but rather on the functioning of components of information processing – how children (as well as adults) actually process information in their heads. This is sometimes called a "cognitive approach."

What changed the senior author's mind was an eye-opening experience he had when he was Director of Graduate Studies in the psychology department at Yale University.

Consider a true story with the names changed.

Alice was, some years ago, an applicant for the graduate program in psychology at Yale (Sternberg, 1985). The program was (and still is) extremely highly selective and admitted only highly gifted students. Alice had achieved stupendously high GRE scores and she also had garnered terrific grades in her four years of college. It seemed reasonable to expect great things of her. But her amazing abstract analytical skills did not translate into long-term success for preparation for the real work of science.

In her first year as a graduate student, her performance was what the GREs predicted. She was an amazing student in the classroom – a star. But science in practice is not about success in the classroom. In order to prepare students for the real work of science, they were expected to formulate and successfully complete scientific research projects. Alice had difficulty coming up with ideas for projects (creative intelligence), and she also had difficulty translating the ideas she did have into practical research projects that could be done in the time available with the resources available (practical intelligence). She was gifted at just what the GREs measure, but not at the skills they were supposed to predict.

The question, of course, was what went wrong? How could the longer-term prediction be so wrong? We believe that, for Alice, as for so many other analytically gifted students, after a school career being rewarded for being gifted analytical thinkers, they deeply bury any creative talents they might have. By the time they get to graduate school, whatever creativity they might have had is deeply buried.

In contrast to Alice was Barbara (Sternberg, 1985), who had relatively poor test scores, at least by Yale standards, and good but not terrific grades. In contrast, she had excellent letters of recommendation trumpeting her creativity and publications showing that she did creative work. From the senior author's point of view, our goal in selecting students was to find creative scientists so she seemed like a great bet. At the same time, none of his colleagues seemed to agree. Her low GRE scores made them skeptical that she could succeed in the Yale graduate program. One full professor pointed out that virtually every student who had succeeded in the graduate program had GRE scores over 650 (163 on the current scale). The senior author replied that this was true, but it was also true that we virtually never accepted students with lower scores so that we were dealing with a self-fulfilling prophecy resulting from a confirmation bias. By only admitting students with high GRE scores, we were assuring that none of the students who succeeded in the program had lower scores.

After Barbara was rejected, the senior author hired her as a research associate. Two years later, she was admitted to the graduate program as the top pick and had a very successful career as a graduate student – and thereafter. Barbara was gifted, but not in the IQ-like sense. Rather, she was extremely creative.

Yet another contrast was Celia (Sternberg, 1985), who had very good but not great grades, very good but not great test scores, and very good but not great recommendations. We admitted her. Her performance in graduate school was very good, although probably not what one would call at the top tier. But the interesting thing was an amazing feat – she was admitted to every graduate school to which she applied. Almost no one so succeeds at that level. The senior author asked himself how she did it. The answer, he realized, was that she was extremely high in practical intelligence, or common sense. She knew how to go into a job interview, give the interviewers what they want, and succeed. And this is an extremely valuable set of skills to have in life.

And that is how the senior author came to realize the incompleteness of analytical skills as a measure of giftedness. Alice, Barbara, and Celia were all three gifted, just in different ways.

So, what happened? Alice, Barbara, and Celia all have had successful careers, much as one might have predicted on the basis of their profiles of giftedness. So, consider creative skills as well as attitudes next!

5.2 Creative Skills and Attitudes

A crucial skill for real-world giftedness is creativity (Bornstein, 2021; Sternberg, 2003) – the ability to generate new and useful or effective ideas (Runco & Jaeger, 2012; Plucker, 2016; Kaufman & Sternberg, 2019). Those children who go on to be gifted in their adult lives usually have a creative contribution to offer. As children, they may be identified as gifted on the basis of the tests that are used for admission to high-IQ societies, such as Mensa (for which one needs an IQ in the 98th percentile), the Prometheus Society (for which one apparently needs an IQ in the 99.997th percentile), and the Mega Society (for which one apparently needs an IQ in the 99.999th percentile) (Evangelisti, N.D.). If there are organizations that have been creatively gifted in their contributions to the world – perhaps some might identify Disney for its continuing novel and engaging entertainment of children or the WHO for its long-term creative contributions to public health – it is not clear that any high-IQ society would be so identified, at least in terms of the definition of adaptive intelligence.

Creativity as defined here refers to genuinely creative work, or the potential to contribute such work, not to inferences made from scores on standardized tests of creativity, such as those of Torrance (1974, 2008), which have generally derived in part from psychometric theories of intelligence, such as that of Guilford (1967, 1988) and Guilford and Hoepfner(1971). The Guilford–Torrance notion of creativity is based on the concept of divergent thinking (Runco, 1991), which is perhaps epitomized by a task in which participants try to think of unusual uses of a paper clip. As with IQ tests, this class of tasks is far afield from the kinds of thinking that are required to solve real problems in the everyday world.

Sternberg and Lubart (1995) suggested that creative thinkers are not merely good at puzzle-like creative tasks. They are people who, above all, are willing to defy the crowd – to go their own way when others are going a different way. On this view, people do not "have" creativity. To a much greater extent, they decide for creativity: creativity is largely an attitude toward life, not just a static ability of some kind (Sternberg, 2000). Once again, giftedness does not inhere so much in the abilities one has as much as it inheres in how one deploys those abilities.

Defying the crowd is easy in principle, but difficult in practice. Most people probably think that, given the choice between doing what is right and what others are doing, they will do the right thing. The problem is that social pressure to do what others are doing is usually strong, and in some places, such as dictatorial countries, the pressures are crushing. In Russia or China or Belarus, defiance of the government may mean, at best, prison, and at worst, death. In neighborhoods that are controlled by violent gangs, the cost of disobeying the gangs can be very high, including the loss of one's life.

The senior author learned a lesson as an adolescent. The style then for young men was to wear tight pants, which supposedly would make young ladies more interested in them. Being claustrophobic and hating anything tight, he wore loose pants. The result was that other students thought he was, at best, a "dork," and at worst, a "dweeb" (whatever the difference happens to be!). He was socially rejected for what, in retrospect, seems to be a very small reason. But in much of life, the stakes are even much higher. If one defies the crowd, one is ostracized.

It turns out that defying the crowd is only one of three attitudes of defiance that underlie much of creativity (Sternberg, 2018a). Creative individuals also need to be able to defy two other sources of ideas and of pressures: themselves and the Zeitgeist.

A major impediment to creativity, and especially gifted levels of creativity, is ourselves. All of us have ideas, including creative ideas, that, at one time or another, have passed their time of maximum creative productivity. One might wish to think that those who are creatively gifted would be the first to let go of their obsolete ideas, but oddly, the pressures on the gifted creative are sometimes greater than the pressures on others. If a gifted individual has had a particularly creative idea and has received a lot of praise for it and perhaps even various kinds of monetary or other rewards or awards, it may be especially hard to let go of the idea, even after one realizes that the idea has become obsolete. For example, gifted individuals may have a scientific theory or an invention that brings them fame and fortune. But scientific theories and inventions do not last forever – they are replaced by better scientific theories and inventions. Yet, the creative individual may have trouble letting go because of various fears – that their next idea will not be as good as the last one; that they will disappoint those who became their followers because of their earlier creative idea; and that they will be ridiculed for convincing people to believe in something that no longer appears to be so valuable. Almost everyone in science – including the authors – knows people who proposed theories when they were in their thirties or forties, and who, when the world moved on, did not move on with it. They stuck with ideas that had once served a purpose but that no longer do. Even children who have a particularly creative idea may become enamored of it and have trouble letting go. There are, of course, some scientific theories or inventions whose value stays the same over very long stretches of time – for example, Charles Darwin's theory of natural selection or the flush toilet. But even both of those have been improved on over time!

Creatively gifted individuals face a third challenge, namely, the Zeitgeist or set of prevailing views of their time. For example, in the days when Sigmund Freud first proposed his theory of psychoanalysis, he had plenty of opposition – Freud defied the crowd. Almost all creative individuals have opposition because their ideas make other people uncomfortable. But harder to escape are the basic assumptions that people of a given era or in a given cultural milieu just take for granted, in the case of the Victorians, for example, the repression of sexuality and the view of women as the "weaker" sex. We all hold so many assumptions that we are not even aware we hold. Part of creative giftedness is questioning the assumptions that others consider sacrosanct or that they may not even be aware they have.

There are many ways to assess creativity (Sternberg, 2017; Plucker et al., 2019). The best, we believe, are not conventional creativity tests, but rather through opportunities for young people to be creative in designing, imagining, supposing, and inventing. People are creative by virtue of the creative things they do in their lives, not by virtue of their performance in artificial testing situations. Moreover, assessment needs to occur over a period of time (Sternberg, 2010). It is not valid to sit someone down and tell them to be creative, on your mark, get set, go. That is not how creativity operates in the real world.

When we have measured creativity in young people (e.g., Sternberg, 2017), we have tried to use problems that resemble those that the young people might encounter in their everyday lives or that might extend their everyday thinking beyond what they have thought about, which is often what creativity requires. For example, students have been given options to draw the beginning of time, draw an advertisement for a boring product, write a short story with a title such as "Trapped" or "The end of the Internet," design a scientific experiment, or speculate on what the world would be like if Germany had won World War II.

Creativity is not fixed (Sternberg, 2016; Plucker et al., 2020). It, like intelligence, can be developed (Sternberg et al., 2008). And it is developed by encouraging a creative attitude toward life. Creativity is, in large part, a decision (Sternberg, 2000). One is willing to defy the crowd, oneself, and the prevailing worldview – the Zeitgeist (Sternberg, 2018a). But one also must be willing to (1) redefine problems that are wrongly conceptualized, (2) recognize when one's thinking is leading nowhere, (3) promote one's creative ideas, (4) take sensible risks, (5) believe in one's own creativity, (6) find within oneself the resilience and stamina to overcome obstacles, (g) be willing to let go of ideas that are not productive, and most of all, (8) recognize that creativity is a way of life, not just something one does in an art or other class in which one is told to "be creative."

5.3 Practical Skills and Attitudes

We often think of giftedness in terms of IQ. But if one reads or listens to media, what stands out (at least to us) is not lack of IQ among public figures but rather lack of common sense. Some of the wackiest politicians went to prestigious colleges and universities. You can pick your choice of leader, but one wonders sometimes what they are thinking. Having a high IQ, or going to a prestigious college, seems not to provide common sense.

5.3.1 Practical Intelligence and Tacit Knowledge

Indeed, over the years, the senior author and his colleagues addressed the question of the relation between common sense and IQ (Sternberg et al., 2000; Sternberg & Hedlund, 2002; Hedlund, 2020). Unlike the Kenya study, these studies were conducted in a postindustrialized setting, the United States. The studies were conducted with children and adults, in a variety of settings, and measuring multiple different aspects of practical intelligence, or common sense. The tests presented real-world problems that required tacit knowledge and either asked participants to say how the problems should be solved or gave various solution options and asked them to rate the quality of the various options. The results were pretty much the same, regardless of how the tests were administered. The correlations of tests of practical intelligence with conventional tests of general intelligence ranged from negative to positive but showed, we believe clearly, that practical intelligence is different from the more academic aspect of intelligence. People can be "gifted" in the sense of having a high IQ and yet have very little common sense. Think, for example, of Dr. Sheldon Cooper, a fictional character from the TV show "The Big Bang Theory." This character is portrayed as an extremely intelligent individual with a highly analytical mind. While Sheldon may possess exceptional intellectual abilities, his social skills and understanding of everyday practical matters are often portrayed as lacking or unconventional. In one episode, his lack of tact is demonstrated when he is interviewing for a prestigious research position at Cal Tech. Instead of networking and showcasing his skills and qualifications, Sheldon exhibits a lack of common sense by insulting the hiring committee and questioning the intelligence of the people interviewing him.

5.3.2 Scientific Reasoning in Practice

For many years, the senior author believed that, although standardized tests might not be all that useful in predicting serious real-world performance, at least they might be useful in assessing the kind of reasoning and problem-solving used by scientists. After all, much of the thinking scientists do is very abstract. And gifted scientists have to think at highly abstract and rarefied levels. But he was wrong.

The demands of the context of schooling and the tasks that schooling presents, whether in the classroom or on tests, just do not well represent the demands of many of the careers that schooling is supposed to prepare students for. One sees this, for example, in law. Many students who get law degrees (J.D.) then take bar exam preparation courses that teach them the law they actually will need to know to become lawyers. One of the senior author's children went to a prestigious law school, and on graduation found that the education she received taught her a lot of great theory but much less actual law.

The experience with Alice described earlier suggested to the senior author that standardized tests, at least those conventionally used in admissions, do not well measure the skills needed for career success. A colleague and the senior author later decided to do a formal study of the issue. Sternberg and Williams (1997) examined the predictive validity of the Graduate Record Examination (GRE) for success in the program of graduate study at Yale in psychological science. Beyond prediction of first-year grades, which in a PhD graduate program matter very little, the GRE generally was only a weak predictor of ratings by professors of students' research-based and teaching-based performance as well as of their analytical, creative, and practical skills. The GRE also was a weak predictor of professors' ratings of the quality of students' doctoral dissertations.

Of course, one might attribute these results to the program being very selective or to its being limited to just one university. But a much broader recent meta-analysis (quantitative compilation of past research) on the GRE found much the same result (Feldon et al., 2023). Almost two-thirds of predictions of academic success were not statistically significant. The magnitudes of observed relations between the GRE and success in school decreased over time. There was some prediction of academic success but the levels of prediction were, arguably, pathetic: GRE scores predicted 2.25 percent of the variance across the various measured outcomes in the study. It predicted only 2.56 percent of variance in first-year graduate GPA, so was not even a good predictor of performance in getting grades.

Tests of predictive validity tend to overestimate the predictive validity of a test because of self-fulfilling prophecies. Students with high test scores are given advantages and special attention that do not go to those with lower test scores. As Rosenthal and Jacobson (2003; see also Weinstein, 2004) found, merely being labeled as smarter leads one to be treated as smarter, with all the benefits that accrue from the label.

The problem, at least at the time Williams and Sternberg did the study, was that the GRE seemed to be pretty much all that was available for predicting success in scientific thinking as it exists in practice, not just in theory. But we now have other tests, and they reveal that testers can construct more comprehensive assessments than the kinds of assessments represented by the SAT, ACT, GRE, and other similar tests.

Sternberg and colleagues conducted a series of studies designed specifically to measure scientific thinking as it exists in practice (Sternberg & Sternberg, 2017; Sternberg et al., 2019, 2020; Sternberg, 2020c). Here is an example we used from a test called Generating Alternative Hypotheses:

"Jasper is interested in the function of water when growing plants. He adds 50 mL of water to the earth in which half of his plants are growing and 150 mL of water to the earth in which the other half of his plants are growing. He notices that plants with the 150 mL of water grow taller than those with the 50 mL of water and claims that water helps the plants to grow even more.

What are some alternative hypotheses regarding why the plants with 150 mL of water grow taller?"

Here is an example from another test, Generating Scientific Experiments:

"Jon believes that radiation from electronic devices such as cell phones and computers negatively influences people's health, especially when the people are at a younger age. However, Jon is not sure how to test this hypothesis.

Please suggest an experimental design to test this hypothesis and describe the experiment in some detail. Assume you have the resources you need to be able to do the experiment."

And here is an example from a test, Drawing Conclusions:

"Tony wanted to see whether exercising for 30 minutes per day would reduce cholesterol levels. He had 10 subjects exercise for at least 30 minutes per day for three weeks and 10 subjects not exercise at all. He also controlled the number of calories all subjects consumed daily. He found that cholesterol levels were reduced for those who did the exercise. He concluded that exercising reduces cholesterol levels and thus lowers the risk of having heart disease.

Is the conclusion correct? Why or why not?"

Note that, unlike in typical standardized testing, the problems require genuine scientific reasoning as it is practiced in a scientific laboratory.

Sternberg and colleagues (Sternberg & Sternberg, 2017; Sternberg et al., 2019, 2020; Sternberg, 2020c) presented items like these to undergraduate students at Cornell University. They also asked the students to answer IQ-test types of items, including number series and classification of letter sets. In number series, students had to complete a series of numbers, and in the classification test they had to say which set of letters did not belong to the other sets. They also asked students to self-report their SAT and/or ACT scores. Sternberg and his collaborators (Sternberg & Sternberg, 2017; Sternberg et al., 2019, 2020) found that whatever conventional standardized tests measure, it was not quality of scientific thinking skills as they are exercised in real science. The tests of scientific reasoning formed one factor, meaning that they were highly related to each other statistically, and the tests of IQ-like skills formed another distinct factor. Thus, scientific-reasoning tests tend to measure one thing, whereas IQ tests another. If one seeks to find the most gifted scientists of the future, one probably will not find them merely through IQ tests and their proxies.

Sternberg and his colleagues extended the research to STEM (science–technology–engineering–mathematics) teaching, which is important in most scientific careers. The students in this study had to complete the measures described here. In addition, they listened to two professors teaching lectures. The two professors purposely taught in a flawed manner. They were specifically instructed to make mistakes, such as being disorganized in their presentations, answering questions in an incomprehensible manner, being sarcastic in answering questions, and showing lack of mastery of the material they were teaching (Sternberg et al., 2017). The students who participated viewed the teaching and were asked to analyze and list the weaknesses and the flaws in the professors' teaching of the lessons. Sternberg and his colleagues found in this study that the students' level of skill in spotting the weaknesses and flaws in the STEM teaching factored with the scientific-thinking assessments but not with the IQ-like assessments. In other words, the tests of STEM reasoning were associated with each other but not with the IQ-like assessments. Thus, scientific research and scientific-teaching skills are not the same, but they are closely related statistically as well as conceptually. To teach science, one has to understand how science works. To analyze teaching in science, one has to understand when the teaching departs from the scientific. In all these studies, it made no difference what science one was analyzing or teaching: the scientific way of thinking crosses disciplinary boundaries.

Sternberg and colleagues also got similar results whether they presented their problems via free response or via multiple-choice. The only difference was that using a multiple-choice format increased the correlations of the scientific-reasoning tests with the IQ-like tests. What this means is that, to some extent, the correlations among IQ-like group tests can be due to common multiple-choice format.

The various studies on scientific thinking as it is actually practiced suggest that the standardized tests for university admissions to STEM programs in use, at least in the United States and perhaps elsewhere, are not ideal for measuring scientific thinking in practice. The risk is that using standardized tests tells schools, colleges, and universities who reasons well and even in a gifted manner in abstract situations, but not who reasons well in concrete scientific situations. We may end up identifying students like Alice, who are gifted in the abstract-analytical domain, but whose strength is in understanding, remembering, and critiquing the ideas of others rather than in generating their own creative ideas and then designing ways to test those ideas. Conventional standardized tests were not designed to measure creative and practical thinking and, apparently, they do not. They are measures of general intelligence and specific knowledge. We should recognize their limitations when we use them. As this Element has pointed out, the world faces pressing problems in science and in other fields. We need to identify as gifted not just people with high general intelligence but also people who can adapt to real situations and apply their gifts effectively to solve problems these situations present.

5.4 Wisdom

Wisdom is defined in many ways (e.g., Ardelt, 2004; Baltes & Staudinger, 2000; Clayton & Birren, 1980; Glück & Weststrate, 2022; Grossmann et al., 2020; Karami et al., 2020), but we define it for our purposes here as the utilization of one's knowledge and skills; to achieve a common good; by balancing one's own, others', and larger interests; over the long as well as the short term; and through the infusion of positive ethical values (Sternberg, 1998a, 2019c). A gifted wise individual, on this view, is one who is exceptionally well able to balance the interests of multiple parties to a conflict situation and find an ethical common good for the long term (Sternberg, 2003b; see also Tirri, 2022).

Wisdom is, we hope obviously, not something one is born with. It is something that develops over time. It requires abilities, certainly, but it also requires experience and learning the right lessons from experience. Experience by itself does not suffice: some people have experience and learn nothing from it or learn the wrong lesson.

One might think that wisdom is a construct that does not apply to children, but it does. Indeed, Malala Yousafzai, who has fought for women's rights in Pakistan and around the world, won the Nobel Peace Prize at age seventeen. Greta Thunberg, who has campaigned worldwide against global climate change, became *Time's Person of the Year* at age sixteen. They are exceptional but not unique. They found a purpose, formulated a plan, and helped to change the world. Thunberg has sometimes mapped out fairly extreme positions on climate change, reflecting her view that there is not a lot of compromise to be made. (For example, if one were to talk about the number of people for whom it would be acceptable to have died from uncontrolled climate change, some might argue that a wise position would be zero rather than, say, a few hundred thousand.)

Whereas high intelligence as measured by IQ tests is in rather large supply worldwide, wisdom is not. It is much easier to think of leaders who probably have a high IQ than of leaders who are wise. Wisdom requires much more than just intelligence, because one needs creativity to come up with wise plans of action, intelligence to ensure that the ideas are good ones, and practical intelligence to implement one's plans and to persuade others of their value.

Moreover, while schools help to develop intelligence, at least in a narrow sense (Ceci, 1996), it is not clear that they do much to develop wisdom. On the contrary, teaching for wisdom has become much less common over the years (Sternberg, 2019b), perhaps because of the demands of standardized testing – which does not assess wisdom – or because the educational establishment just values wisdom less.

It is possible to teach for wisdom (Lipman, 1987; Sternberg et al., 2007, 2011; Ferrari & Kim, 2019; Sternberg & Hagen, 2019), but no one would say it is easy, and it is not. In the end, one can teach what wisdom is, teach why it is important, provide role models, have children model wise behavior, and learn about wise and unwise decisions. But acting wisely is a decision all students, including gifted students, have to decide to make.

6 Aspects of Giftedness

Giftedness comes in many varieties, not all of them good.

6.1 Foolishness and Dark and Toxic Giftedness

Regarding wisdom, the problem is that not everyone who is gifted chooses to be wise. Some choose to be foolish, despite their intellectual gifts (Sternberg, 2004, 2005, 2018b). Intellectual and other forms of giftedness do not provide any protection from foolishness. On the contrary, often people who are gifted are unusually susceptible to being foolish precisely because they do not believe they are or can be foolish. They do not take precautions because they just know foolishness could not happen to them. But foolishness has nothing to do with intellect. People who are foolish believe that (1) if they have an idea, it must be good or even great; (2) it's all about them – the world revolves about them, or at least, it should; (3) they are omniscient or close to it – far more knowledgeable than experts, no matter how fancy the experts' credentials; (4) they are omnipotent – they can do whatever they want; (5) they are invulnerable – no matter what they do, no one will be able successfully to call them to account; (6) if things seem to be going off track, they should just keep doing what they are doing because eventually, without doubt, they will succeed because they are who they are.

So, the foolish stumble through life. If they are both sufficiently narcissistic and sufficiently persuasive or even charismatic, they may be able to carry on their failed act for a long time. The problem is that they not only carry themselves down, they also carry others down with them. And then a lot of people "own" the message that the foolish people created.

Worse are the toxic people – those who not only lack wisdom but also are in a sense the opposite of wise (Sternberg, 2018b). They poison things. They may poison interpersonal or international relationships or just about anything they touch. Toxically gifted leaders are never recognized as such by their followers, not because the followers could not recognize it, but because they do not want to, whatever their IQs; and many of the followers of toxic leaders have high IQs and follow the toxic leaders because they see gain for themselves personally. In the United States, as of 2023, you can still identify a leader as toxic; in many other countries, such as Russia, China, or Belarus, if you say so, at best, you go to prison, at worst, you die. Dictators of these countries cannot allow their authority to be questioned for the fear that questioning will become an epidemic or even a pandemic. In such dictatorships, in *1984* (Orwell, 1950) fashion, the gifted are the ones who do what they are told, regardless of how stupid or immoral it is. And they know what they do is wrong, which is how the toxic leaders get the followers to stay with them. The followers become compromised and have little other choice.

Are leaders like Putin, Xi, or Orban in Hungary "gifted"? Of course, they are: they have all of the characteristics in the pentagonal theory of identification of the gifted. How many people can acquire and then keep power, despite the number of enemies such leaders have? They pull off a feat that very few people in the world could pull off. Not all the toxic leaders are gifted. Alexander Lukashenko of Belarus is a toady: he is in power so long as Putin wants him and will lose it when Putin finds someone else who can do the dirty work better. But it is better to face these things than to repeat the mistake of the twentieth century with Adolf Hitler, when people kept trying to find excuses until there were no more excuses to be found. And even today, there are people who follow Hitler: sects do not necessarily die with their toxic leaders.

Why do people become toxic or even toxically gifted? Many are dark-triad individuals: they are narcissistic, Machiavellian, and psychopathic (Paulhus & Williams, 2002). Many of their followers share these characteristics, and others, like Steve Bannon in the United States, are just haters: they are intellectually brilliant but need individuals and groups to hate and, to fulfill their ambitions, they need other people to join them in their hate (Sternberg, 2003a; Sternberg & Sternberg, 2008), the basis for Oceania in *1984* (Orwell, 1950).

Some readers might wonder what a discussion such as this one is doing in an Element on childhood giftedness. The answer is that, although we all have the best hopes for people identified as "gifted," some will follow antisocial and even toxic paths. Some people in almost any group will do so, including even people who spend their lives in the clergy supposedly doing good. Programs for the gifted could take the attitude that what children do with their gifts when they grow up is not the business of the schools. But they also could take the attitude that they should teach not only academic content but also how to deploy that content in a way that will make the world a better, not a worse, place. After all, talent development is a dynamic process in which giftedness is undoubtedly influenced by both the individual's interaction with their surrounding environment and the specific challenges the individual encounters during the developmental journey. Educators should then take a holistic approach and develop the gifts and talents that will make the world better for all. That is the position of the authors of this Element.

6.2 Intellectual Integrity

We have argued elsewhere that at least as important as intellect in life is intellectual integrity (Sternberg, 2021c; Sternberg & Lubart, 2022). Intellectual integrity comprises two parts.

The first principle is a striving for the internal coherence of one's thinking. All people live with some level of cognitive dissonance (Festinger & Carlsmith, 1959). They have incompatible thoughts, such as that they are a moral person despite overdeclaring deductions on their income tax or lifting something from a supermarket that, well, they think, hardly will make any difference to anyone. People often know they should think morally but do not get around to it (Ambrose, 2022). Sometimes the incompatibility grows and becomes malignant, as, for example, when a person is opposed to racism but allows or even encourages it in themselves because members of one race, they believe, really are inferior, and besides, they are a threat to everyone else. The clergy who abuse children and the self-declared patriotic Russian soldiers who commit genocide in Ukraine or elsewhere live with internal incoherence that has become malignant.

People who live with extreme internal incoherence may be just not very bright and so not recognize the incoherence, or they may be intellectually adept but still not recognize the incoherence of the thinking or want to deal with it. Managers of concentration camps around the world, past and present, often go home to their families and live relatively normal lives at night and on weekends. But part of gifted education should be helping children recognize incoherence in thinking, deal with it, and decide whether the incoherence is morally sustainable. Wells that become contaminated often become so little by little. Minds can become contaminated little by little as well. For those who are gifted, applying one's gifts in an ethical manner can be a slippery slope (Sternberg, 2011). The senior author asked a former colleague of his who worked in a company that he described as unethical why he stayed there. The colleague answered that if he had known when he applied for the position, how unethical it was, he never would have applied for the job. But he realized only slowly how unethical it was and how it compromised the people who worked there. His situation was like that of Mitch McDeere in the novel *The Firm* (Grisham, 2009). The partners in the law firm corrupted associates little by little, until the associates were thoroughly compromised. The associates, like many people who become corrupt, were gifted. Children need to learn how to make ethical choices. No matter what our education, we all will make some mistakes, including some big ones. The challenge is then to find one's way out of whatever the morass is that we may find ourselves in.

The second principle is external coherence – that what one believes one knows corresponds to what is out there. Kant (1781/2008) recognized, long ago, that we never can know reality in itself. It is always filtered by our perceptions, emotions, and motivations. But there is a difference between trying one's best to act on facts and trying to invent facts to fit the reality one would like. In the United States, democracy has been slipping (Albright, 2018; Levitsky & Ziblatt, 2018; Mounk, 2018) because of the insistence of politicians with ideological agendas on reshaping people's perceptions of reality to fit the politicians' ideologies, or often, conceptions of how they can attain and maintain power. Some politicians are charismatic and gifted at acquiring followers. But they are also toxic, taking down a country to serve their own interests. Regrettably, this is happening today in Israel as we write. A leader with a mixed past seems intent on destroying the country to stay in power and out of prison (TOI Staff, 2023).

6.3 Transformational versus Transactional Giftedness

We have argued that society is making a mistake in the way it defines giftedness. It is identifying as "gifted" primarily people who are conventionally smart. If one considers the staggering problems facing the world today, those who are gifted in that conventional sense do not seem to be making much headway, at least in combating global climate change, pollution, violence, gross income disparities, weapons of mass destruction, and many other very dangerous problems. What is wrong?

Giftedness in our society is viewed largely as transactional: the gifted child turns in a high level of performance on some kind of task, usually an academic one, and then is labeled as "gifted." In return, the now "gifted" individual is expected to continue to perform at a high level – to get good grades, high test scores, prestigious college and university admissions, attain a well-paying job, perhaps win a few awards along the way. Their gifts are expected to show in their income and standard of living. Today, societal reward-seeking can become a cynical game, where colleges and universities start admitting students because of the resources their parents can donate or because of the hope that future graduates will themselves become generous donors to the institution. The deal is a "tit-for-tat" one, where the gifted person provides something and gets something in return; this kind of transaction can be contrasted with a second kind of giftedness, transformational giftedness (Sternberg, 2020d, 2020e, 2021d; Sternberg et al., 2021, 2022).

Transformational giftedness is the utilization of one's gifts to change the world – to make it a better place, not just for oneself or people whom one perceives to be like oneself, but for the common good. Transformationally gifted individuals make the world better. They may also be transactionally gifted, in that often transformation involves a series of successful transactions with others whom one wants to recruit to one's metaphorical "team." But the goal is to transform the world. Transformational leaders who succeed in their jobs often are what we here are calling transformationally gifted (Bass et al., 1996; Bass, 1998; Bass & Riggio, 2006).

Toxic leaders are pseudo-transformationally gifted (see also Bass, 1998; Bass et al., 1996). They are individuals who pretend to use their gifts to make the world a better place, when, in fact, they are interested only in making the world better for themselves. We need to lead young people down a path of transformational giftedness, not down a pseudo-transformational path.

7 Giftedness as a Result of Adversity

In previous sections, we established that a long-standing tradition has involved labeling people as gifted based exclusively or largely on IQ. Yet we know that IQ as the sole or even principal indicator of giftedness is flawed in many ways and has led to systemic exclusion of certain populations, including but not limited to Black, Indigenous, and People of Color (BIPOC), people from low-income backgrounds, and people with specific disabilities. Moreover, we have established a compound effect that makes it more difficult for people from certain backgrounds to be recognized as gifted. These backgrounds include, but are not limited to, people who are non-White, who are noncisgender, who have grown up in poverty, or who live with specific disabilities. Yet, when we expand contemporary conceptions of giftedness and talent and trade our deficit perspective for a strength-based one, we may find that historically excluded populations are more inclined to demonstrate giftedness and to achieve eminence because of the adversity with which they have coped. Such a perspective acknowledges that giftedness is not a property of an individual, but rather of an interaction among an individual, a task or set of tasks, and a situation or set of situations (Sternberg, 2021b, 2023b; Sternberg et al., 2022; Sternberg & Preiss, 2022; Tromp & Sternberg, 2022). In this section, we explore adversity from a strength-based perspective to highlight hidden strengths that may develop as a result of adversity, yet are overlooked and underappreciated in traditional approaches to gifted identification and programming.

7.1 Let's Not Ignore Reality

Applying a strength-based lens to the discussion of talent development in light of adversity, rather than a deficit one, is essential to promote giftedness and talent among people who have experienced adversity. This strength-based focus allows us to acknowledge the valuable skills and assets people develop in response to their experiences. However, it is also important to recognize that growing up with adversity, in particular, systemic adversity, such as effects of poverty and racism, presents very real challenges that are difficult to overcome, no matter how resilient a person is. For example, children from low-income backgrounds are more likely to experience harsh early environments that can negatively affect aspects of brain development associated with school readiness skills (Hair et al., 2015). These children are also more likely to live in under-resourced communities and with financial struggles that may affect their parents' ability to promote cognitive stimulation, which in turn may result in children entering school with less advanced vocabularies and with knowledge gaps that put them up to a year behind their peers (Miller et al., 2019). Because poverty tends to be a systemic problem, children from low-income families may accumulate disadvantages over time that result in fewer opportunities for talent development throughout the school career (see, for example, Plucker et al., 2010; Plucker, Hardesty et al., 2013; Olszewski-Kubilius & Corwith, 2018). Ignoring these challenges can perpetuate marginalization and discrimination. Therefore, we want to be very clear that, although we focus on strengths developed through adversity and argue that they may contribute to positive development, we also recognize the necessity of appropriate resources and opportunities for successful positive development.

An experience of the senior author is relevant. On a sabbatical, he and his wife enrolled their triplets in a German Gymnasium (secondary school). Their home school in New York requested that, once the children returned to New York, the German school send the children's grades back to the school in New York. The author and his wife argued that this was not a fair request, because, although the children are bilingual, their level of German and their acculturation into Germany would not be at the same level as that of the children who grew up in Germany. After registering what seemed to the author like a righteous objection, the author realized that the situation to which he objected is very similar to the situation many millions of immigrant children and children of diverse cultures encounter every day in their schooling. They are judged among students whose native language and enculturation give those students a tremendous advantage, but the students with different backgrounds get little or no indulgence when they are judged. The author was requesting for his children a privilege that very few culturally and linguistically diverse children get. What are their chances of being identified as gifted when they must struggle just to understand what is going on around them?

7.2 Hidden Talents

Childhood adversity, including familial adversity, such as parental substance abuse, and systemic adversity like institutional discrimination or poverty, is often approached from a deficit perspective. Researchers have well established vulnerabilities and weaknesses that may result from childhood adversity. For example, childhood adversity may negatively affect language development, executive functioning, memory, and social-emotional processing (Ursache & Noble, 2016). Additionally, children who have experienced adversity may lack the resources and opportunities to help them develop their gifts and talents (Olszewski-Kubilius & Corwith, 2018). But what about strengths associated with childhood adversity?

The idea of thriving in the face of adversity is not new. Eisenstadt (1978) examined 699 eminent people and determined that people whose parent(s) died when they were young were more likely to achieve eminence in their fields than those who did not have one or both parents die when they were young. Later, Simonton (1999) suggested that early adversity may increase creative eminence. Social and cognitive skills that develop in response to adversity are not as well studied as they ideally might be (Ellis et al., 2020, 2023; Frankenhuis et al., 2020; Ellis, Abrams, et al., 2023). Ellis and colleagues (2020, 2023) have referred to these skills and strengths as "hidden talents" because they tend to be overlooked.

In the Hidden Talents Framework, Ellis and colleagues (2023) proposed that individuals who have experienced adversity may develop hidden talents and strengths as a result of their challenges. Adversity can serve as a catalyst for developing adaptive skills and coping mechanisms, such as resilience, persistence, adaptability, and empathy. It has been well-established that children facing adversity may lack supportive relationships, resources, and opportunities in their early life and school career. The environmental factors they are exposed to may negatively affect their talent development, at least early on. While we do not deny these possible negative effects, there is light amidst the dark that tends to be ignored when approaching adversity from a deficit perspective only. For example, children who grow up in "working class" families, with parents who work multiple jobs or long hours, may lack parental presence. However, they may also grow up in a family where a strong work ethic is modeled and expected. Observing this level of dedication may positively influence their own work ethic and dedication (Hardy et al., 2017).

Similarly, the scarcity mindset that may come with growing up in poverty can cause anxiety. Still, it may also develop a spirit of striving for achievement that may drive talent development. Children may be less cognitively stimulated as a result of limited financial resources, resulting in a lack of learning opportunities in the form of books and toys to play with, but a lack of resources may force children to become creative and practice problem-solving frequently (Sternberg, 1997; Simonton, 1999). Furthermore, Sternberg (2019d) has argued that individuals who grow up in challenging environments may develop wisdom as a result of their experiences. When used in the broader sense (i.e., any event or experience perceived as challenging or threatening to goals or well-being), adversity in some degree may be essential for success (Hardy et al., 2017; Sarkar & Fletcher, 2017). Thus, childhood adversity can have both positive and negative effects on giftedness and talent.

Walters and Gardner (1984) wrote of the importance of crystallizing experiences in talent development. Such experiences are ones that profoundly affect the course of a lifetime and often of a person's later contributions. The senior author of this Element had such an experience when he performed disastrously on IQ tests as a child. As a result, many of his teachers considered him to be intellectually challenged. He decided at that point to study intelligence as a career, which he proceeded to do. He turned an adverse experience into a life pursuit. Similarly, the junior author had to repeat third grade. To this day, she remembers getting the news and thinking her mother was joking. This decision not only affected her self-perception but also led teachers and caring adults to underestimate her. So much so, that although she managed to graduate elementary and secondary school on time, despite being held back, she was advised not to bother pursuing a college degree because of her average high school grades. While in college, these experiences led her to study motivation and underachievement. She went on to obtain a PhD in educational psychology and has published books on underachievement so that teachers may better understand and serve these students' needs.

7.3 Holistic Talent Development Models and Multifactorial Conceptions of Giftedness

What strengths are associated with adversity and how can they positively affect talent development? To recognize possible strengths associated with childhood adversity, we need to operate from a holistic perspective on giftedness and talent and move away from a sole focus on analytical skills. Talent development models, such as the Differentiated Model of Giftedness and Talent (Gagne, 2018) and the Talent Development Mega Model (Subotnik et al., 2011), as well as multifactorial conceptions of giftedness, such as the Augmented Theory of Successful Intelligence (Sternberg, 2020f) and the Three Ring Conception of Giftedness (Renzulli, 1978, 2016), generally recognize that talent development is a dynamic process that involves a complex interaction between individual factors (e.g., cognitive abilities, personality traits, and motivation) and environmental factors (e.g., family support, educational opportunities, and cultural expectations). In other words, being smart or otherwise possessing a set of seemingly gifted traits is not enough for successful talent development that will translate into high-level achievement or demonstrated excellence. Beyond intelligence, creativity, social skills, and plain hard work are often requirements for high-level achievement, along with supportive relationships, mentorship, resources, and opportunity. These holistic perspectives are important when discussing giftedness in light of childhood adversity for two reasons. First, childhood adversity such as poverty is associated with lower IQ, reduced language proficiency, and impaired executive functioning (e.g., Duncan et al., 2017; Ursache & Noble, 2016). Thus, overreliance on cognitive ability as the central tenet of giftedness and talent is perpetuating inequity and marginalization of people with adverse childhood experiences, when they may have hidden talents in noncognitive domains (e.g., expression or interpretation of emotions) or broader cognitive domains not measured by IQs (e.g., creativity; Ellis et al., 2020). They may be excellent solvers of complex problems, regardless of IQ (Dörner, 1986, 1990; Dörner & Funke, 2017). Second, these holistic models emphasize that natural ability does not automatically develop into giftedness or talent. For giftedness to be realized in action requires dedication and hard work. So, motivation takes up a central role in the talent development process; and it just so happens that motivation is highly relevant in the context of what makes childhood adversity a possible catalyst for giftedness.

7.4 Adversity as a Motivational Trigger

Motivation drives our actions. It inspires us to work toward our goals and persist through challenges. Motivation is a complex phenomenon influenced by multiple interrelated variables such as values, expectations, perceptions of the environment and oneself, and basic psychological needs (Ryan & Deci, 2017; Eccles & Wigfield, 2020). Most talent development models address motivation in terms of interest, intrinsic motivation, persistence, and self-efficacy (e.g.,

Gagné, 2018; Subotnik et al., 2011). Renzulli's (1978, 2016) Three Ring Conception of Giftedness focuses on task commitment, and Sternberg's (2020f) concept of successful intelligence captures motivation in two ways: resilience and intention. The concepts of resilience and successful intelligence overlap in that resilience is the ability to persevere and overcome adversity, whereas successful intelligence is the ability to know when and how to adapt to, shape, and select appropriate environments. Motivation can also be seen as intention, as is the case with Sternberg's transformational giftedness (2020d) and the wisdom component of the augmented theory of successful intelligence (2020g). How adversity can influence intention, transformation, and wisdom will be addressed in Section 7.6. First, we will explore adversity as a motivational trigger for talent development.

Surviving and coping with childhood adversity requires a level of resilience and persistence that may be essential for achieving long-term success and eminence in any field or talent domain. Resilience is a skill that can be learned and developed over time. When growing up in adverse circumstances, children may have many opportunities to learn and practice resilience. Successful people with adverse childhood experiences are often highly resilient because of the opportunities afforded by adverse experiences (Seery, 2011; Ellis et al., 2023). However, positive adaptation to adversity is key to success, not simply the experience of adversity. Positive adaptation to adversity has positive effects via the creation of a sense of mastery over past adversity (Seery, 2011). Past adversity may positively affect people's expectations for success in the face of new adverse experiences (Seery, 2011). Positive adaption to adversity also may foster perceived control (Seery, 2011), which in turn promotes self-determination. Finally, many successful people who overcame adverse childhood experiences also did so with the help of a supportive network and meaningful relationships or mentorship (Sarkar et al., 2015; Hardy et al., 2017). This experience may foster useful social skills and a belief that they can successfully establish the effective social network necessary for advanced talent development (Seery, 2011).

Beyond resilience, adversity may result in strong task commitment by igniting a desire to excel at high levels. Some examples, from a study among Olympic athletes, include wanting to achieve to please people, to make parents proud, and out of a sense of injustice (Sarkar et al., 2015). Depending on the level and type of trauma, Sarkar and colleagues (2015) found that adversity may result in striving for superior achievement out of an urgent need to prove something. From her clinical experience, the junior author noted that this may transfer to gifted people with specific disabilities. When people experience a perceived injustice, such as being excluded from opportunities based on a disability, this adverse experience may turn into an obsession with proving people wrong. Striving to become a top performer can then become a central part of one's being (raison d'être; Sarkar et al., 2015). If the striving becomes obsessive, it also can become psychologically unhealthy. Some people may also be able to leverage survival instincts and adaptive intelligence developed from mastering childhood adversity and use them to their advantage in their talent development. Instincts to avoid danger may lead to a heightened awareness of possible obstacles or threats. Proactively identifying these obstacles and risks may allow for mitigating the risks. Similarly, continually lacking resources may position an individual to be able to seek out resources or accept and utilize opportunities to the fullest when those opportunities present themselves (Weston & Imas, 2018). Finally, prolonged exposure to stress that results in successful adaption to that stress may allow individuals to better regulate emotional and physiological stress responses and render them better equipped to perform under pressure. These abilities may contribute to the resilience and persistence essential for talent development. Thus, in some ways, adverse childhood experiences may trigger motivation.

7.5 Creativity as a Function of Adversity

The expression "beauty from pain" refers to the popular belief that something positive or beautiful can emerge from a painful or challenging experience. The expression is often used to refer to personal growth or artistic work that results from adverse experiences. We have already addressed how adversity can promote personal growth through motivation, but there is a common belief that adversity may also enhance creativity. One relatively well-researched area is the connection between artistic expression and adversity. The stereotype of the tortured artist is a very old one.

Consider Vincent van Gogh, the Dutch painter who suffered from depression and mental illness and captured his struggles in paintings such as "The Starry Night." Sylvia Plath, the American poet and writer who famously captured her struggles in her novel *The Bell Jar*, and eventually committed suicide at age thirty, and Frida Kahlo, the Mexican artist who experienced lifelong physical and emotional pain that inspired her famous self-portraits, are other well-known examples of tortured artists. More recently, Tupac Shakur and Eminem, both American rappers who are known for their raw and emotional lyrics capturing their traumatic life experiences, embody the tortured-artist stereotype. It is not just a stereotype. The average life span of American pop, rock, and rap stars is forty-five; in Europe, they make it, on average, only to thirty-nine (Neporent, 2012).

Artists, writers, and musicians tend to draw on their personal experiences of hardship and adversity to create works that are deeply meaningful and impactful (Wittkower & Wittokower, 2006). In this way, adversity can become a catalyst for creative expression and provide a way for individuals to process and make sense of their experiences. People who report greater levels of posttraumatic growth also report greater levels of creative expression (e.g., writing, painting, and music (Forgeard, 2013)). Indeed, engaging in creative tasks can help to remedy childhood adversity (Drus et al., 2014) and such engagement can function as a powerful coping strategy for people who face adverse circumstances (Bryant-Davis, 2005; Van Lith, 2015). Creating can provide a healthy outlet for emotions and help people make sense of their experiences (Kramer, 1971; Malchiodi, 2011). For example, Malchiodi's (2011) theory of art in therapy and Edith Kramer's (1971) theory of art as therapy both highlight the importance of art as a tool for healing and self-expression in the therapeutic process.

Both theories emphasize the importance of the creative process, or art-making, as a way for people to express and explore their emotions, reduce stress, develop a deeper self-understanding, and make sense of their experiences. According to Kramer (1971), engaging in art-making provides a safe and nonjudgmental space to engage in therapeutic work. In both theories, the end result or creative product is not important. Healing happens as a result of the process of creating itself. Among other things, art allows the use of symbolism to draw meaning out of experiences and to gain new insights. Through artistic expression, people can express and discover themselves by accessing conscious and unconscious emotions and experiences. Art provides a way to express and process emotion and may also help people find meaning and purpose in their experiences, similar to how the Olympic athletes develop a dedication to their sport as a way to cope with adversity (Sarakar et al., 2015; Hardy et al., 2017).

Creativity is, of course, broader than performing or visual arts. It captures original and novel thinking and problem-solving in wide variety of contexts and talent domains. Adversity may contribute to creativity by promoting outside-the-box thinking and problem-solving, in general (e.g., Simonton, 1999). Growing up in adverse circumstances, people are faced with limitations and constraints that force them to think creatively to find ways to achieve their goals (Tromp & Sternberg, 2022). For example, Zimbabweans developed an informal economy during their period of colonization to transform their crisis condition into one of creative survival (Weston & Imas, 2018). When the people of Zimbabwe faced extreme poverty and traditional businesses were no longer sustainable, people used creative survival tactics to establish an entirely informal economy where goods and services were traded on small scales. Although not without its challenges, this adaptation allowed people to maintain a sense of agency and to find opportunities in a system of oppression. People learned new skills, took advantage of opportunities, repurposed "worthless" materials, leveraged storytelling and persuasion to navigate the difficulties of doing business on the streets, and so much more. These ongoing experiences with problem-solving can cultivate creativity and innovation that may transfer to all areas of life.

Thus, creativity may be enhanced through adversity because it may be used to cope with adverse circumstances through creative expression or creative problem-solving.

7.6 Wisdom as a Function of Adversity

Childhood adversity can be challenging and difficult to deal with, but it can also be a source of great wisdom and growth (Staudinger & Glück, 2011; Weststrate & Glück, 2017; Jayawickreme et al., 2021). The theory of adaptive intelligence, which includes analytical, creative, and practical intelligence as well as wisdom, along with the concept of transformational giftedness, highlights that it is not just about what gifts you possess but also about how you use them (Sternberg, 2021). Wisdom and transformational giftedness involve using your abilities to make positive contributions to society. So, wisdom and transformational giftedness bring a new perspective to motivation by moving away from motivation as a catalyst for commitment to action and on to motivation as the intention behind the action. This kind of motivation is relevant to highlight because adverse childhood experiences may promote the development of empathy, compassion, and perspective-taking (Ellis et al., 2023), which are foundational to wisdom and transformational giftedness.

In general, many people believe wisdom stems from life experience, both positive and negative. Yet, we also know that not all individuals with adverse life experiences are wise. For this reason, the research on the relation between wisdom and adversity is perhaps the most inconclusive, with regard to empirical evidence, among all associations discussed so far. Some studies report little to no change in wisdom as a consequence of experiencing and overcoming adversity (Dorfman et al., 2022), whereas others have found empirical correlations, but they are mediated by underlying personality traits influencing the relation between wisdom and adversity (Jayawickreme et al., 2017).

Some theories about adversity propose that positive self-perception and positive revisions to life narratives enable people to endure positive change and personal growth from adversity and trauma (Pals & McAdams, 2004). So, in terms of wisdom, it has been argued that people have to view their adverse circumstances, such as the loss of a loved one, natural disasters, and financial hardship, as opportunities for developing wisdom or learning other lessons (Jayawickreme et al., 2017). Thus, to experience personal growth from adversity, engaging in self-reflection is essential (Weststrate & Glück, 2017). Jayawickreme and colleagues (2017) found that people high in personality traits such as openness and extraversion are more likely to view adverse experiences as opportunities for personal growth and, as such, are more likely to gain wisdom from adversity. People who engage in exploratory processing of difficult experiences are also more likely to develop wisdom than those who avoid or suppress such experiences (Weststrate & Glück, 2017). By reflecting on past experiences, individuals can gain new insights, develop new coping strategies, and better understand their own values and beliefs. Perceptions of adversity subsequently affect how likely the stressful life event will be perceived as an opportunity for the development of wisdom.

Wisdom is a complex and multifaceted concept. Depending on the definition of wisdom, many factors can contribute to the development of wisdom, but a common denominator of theories of wisdom tends to be that wisdom is linked to empathy, compassion, and prosocial behavior (Karami et al., 2020; Glück & Weststrate, 2022). When people go through adverse experiences themselves, they may be more likely to understand and relate to others who are going through similar situations. For that reason, empathy may be heightened among people who have experienced adversity (Lim & DeSteno, 2016). These kinds of experiences can lead to a greater concern for others and may foster prosocial behavior (Vollhardt & Staub, 2011).

Diverse adverse experiences may lead to increased prosocial attitudes. For example, increased prosocial behavior is found among those mourning the loss of a spouse (Brown et al., 2008), stroke survivors (Gillen, 2005), and victims of sexual abuse and other interpersonal violence (Grossman et al., 2006). Prosocial behavior and altruism benefit in-group members, such as friends and family or those who suffered a similar experience (Gillen, 2005; Brown et al., 2008), but Vollhardt and Staub (2011) found that the relation between adversity and prosocial attitudes also extends to outgroups.

However, increased empathy and prosocial behavior do not always occur because of adversity. The type of adversity and the length of exposure may affect the association between adversity and empathy. Fourie and colleagues (2019) found that greater experienced social adversity (i.e., discrimination based on income, gender, and race) among children in South Africa was associated with reduced reported compassion. Additionally, destructive and antisocial responses to victimization are not uncommon (Dodge et al., 1990; Chaitin & Steinberg, 2008). When dealing with chronic adversity, people may be too focused on their own suffering to empathize or recognize suffering among others (Chaitin & Steinberg, 2008). Or if they do recognize and empathize with the suffering of others, they may need to attend to their own needs before helping others.

Thus, depending on the type of adversity and whether the adverse experience is perceived as an opportunity for personal growth, adversity may cultivate greater wisdom.

7.7 Courage as a Function of Adversity

Heroism as the act of displaying courage is often intertwined with adversity. Comic book fans know that superheroes are often born out of adversity. Adversity is an essential element of the superhero narrative, as it creates tension and conflict that drives the story forward (Rank, 2004). Without adversity, there would be no need for superheroes to rise to the occasion and demonstrate their bravery, intelligence, and strength. They are faced with challenges that test their physical and mental limits, and they must use their unique abilities and skills to overcome these challenges. Whether fighting off supervillains, saving the world from destruction, or dealing with personal struggles, superheroes are constantly pushed to their limits.

Art imitates life in that this is the case for many real-life heroes as well. Martin Luther King Jr., Nelson Mandela, and Malala Yousafzai are but three famous examples demonstrating the courage that is not only needed to overthrow systemic adversity but that also grows from the adversity.

Courage is essential for both personal and professional successes in life. Gifted individuals often face unique challenges, including the social pressure to conform, fear of failure, and risk of being ostracized for their intellectual abilities (Sternberg, 2022b). So, courage becomes an essential part of making a positive difference in the world. People who overcome adversity report feeling more confident, empowered, and courageous as a result of their experiences (Mulé, 2018; Smith et al., 2020; Omar, 2022). When individuals face adversity, they are often forced to confront their fears, overcome obstacles, and develop personal strengths and resilience. This experience of overcoming adversity then can be leveraged to develop courage.

In light of increased societal adversity across the world, there is an increasing need for everyone, but especially gifted and talented people, to stand up for good causes and successfully navigate challenges that inevitably come with standing up for one's beliefs. However, courage is not without risk, especially considering societal adversity (Sternberg, 2022b). Around the world, there is evidence of a shift toward autocracy (Albright, 2018; Levitsky & Ziblatt, 2018; Mounk,

2018). Many countries are falling under autocratic and corrupt regimes through fraudulent elections, where opposing the regime may result in imprisonment, torture, and death. Look for example at the many people who have died just in the past few years while standing up for their freedom in Iran, Afghanistan, Russia, Sudan, and many other countries (Mackintosh & Elbagin, 2019; Avetisyan, 2021; Human Rights Watch, 2021; Amnesty International, 2022). Courage may at times involve real risks to one's health and safety.

This self-sacrificing component of courage demonstrates why courage is not only needed to overcome adversity but also grows from adversity. Consider the current situation in Iran. Iranian women have faced significant challenges in their quest for equality, freedom, and basic human rights for decades. Women's rights have been restricted by the Iranian government, and women have been subject to discrimination, harassment, and violence. However, in the face of adversity, many Iranian women have demonstrated courage by speaking out against injustice, advocating for change, and standing up for their rights. Most recently, the repression of women has sparked a civil revolution, commonly known as the "woman, life, freedom" movement. Although Iranian women have been fighting for their rights since the late twentieth century, it was not until recent years when mandatory veiling laws have resulted in the heavily publicized arrest, torture, and killing of several Iranian women, including Mahsa Amini. As a result of her death, the protest movement reached a global effort.

Although not a necessary factor, desperation can be a powerful motivator for civil revolution. The women of Iran became increasingly desperate for change and the sense of injustice became so strong that it cultivated courageous action. The adversity reached a point where people accepted the "or die trying" mindset. Their situation sparked a sense of urgency and commitment that superseded fear for personal safety and fear of self-sacrifice. We see how this pattern of courage developed from adversity reoccurs in a variety of human rights movements and civil revolutions, including the Gay Pride movement and the Black Lives Matter movement in the United States.

Courage comes in many shapes and sizes. It can emanate from first responders who risk their lives to save others, or creators sharing their controversial ideas with the public, or activists who stand up for their beliefs. Regardless of how it is manifest, courage can be cultivated through adversity and is in many ways necessary to overcome adversity.

7.8 But Adversity Is Not Enough

It is not merely the experience of adversity but the positive adaptation to that adversity that provides an important catalyst for talent development. So, adversity does not guarantee successful talent development. In some cases, facing adversity can actually stifle motivation, creativity, wisdom, and more. Adversity is more likely to have negative effects if stress and pressure become overwhelming or if one becomes stuck in negative thought patterns.

Furthermore, although the ability to positively adapt to adversity plays an important role in successful talent development, it is not the sole determining factor. Those people with adverse childhood experiences who can achieve success tend to be more resilient, dedicated, and creative (e.g., Ellis et al., 2023), but those who benefit also tend to have one or more supportive relationships and access to opportunities for education and training (e.g., Hardy et al., 2017). For example, research on elite athletes, including Olympians, found that negative critical or traumatic events alone were insufficient to develop the attributes necessary to become elite athletes (Hardy et al., 2017). Hardy and colleagues further found that for those who benefited from adversity, negative critical events, such as divorced parents or learning difficulties, occurred in close temporal proximity to the experience of a positive critical event, such as an inspirational coach or success experience, within or linked to the talent domain. This temporal proximity between the negative and positive critical events was likely an important factor in preventing the negative outcomes typically associated with negative critical foundational events. So, although adversity may act as a motivational trigger (Howells & Fletcher, 2015) and, as such, fuels ambition or effort (Sarkar et al., 2015), it is not without risk of negative side effects. Furthermore, in some cases, adversity as a motivational trigger can have a "dark side" in that it may result in "a single-minded, narcissistic desire to prove one's worth" (Sarkar et al. 2015, p. 478) with little regard for the cost to others or oneself.

In brief, there may be an optimal level of adversity or an ideal balance between adverse experiences and protective factors determining who overcomes and who succumbs to the adversity.

8 Giftedness among People with Disabilities

Although, historically, giftedness and disability were thought of as mutually exclusive, it has been well-established that the two can, in fact, co-occur (e.g., Foley Nicpon et al., 2011; Gliman et al., 2013; McCallum et al., 2013). Individuals with high cognitive ability or who demonstrate talent in one or more areas and who also possess learning, emotional, physical, sensory, and/or developmental disability are referred to as twice- or multi-exceptional (Foley Nicpon et al., 2011). Similar to the research and literature on adversity, the study of people with disabilities has often been conducted from a deficit perspective. We still have limited knowledge of the strengths of people with specific disabilities and those who are twice- or multi-exceptional. Yet, more and more CEOs, senior executives, and artists openly discuss having disabilities and how their struggles made them successful. For example, real estate mogul and Shark Tank cast member Barbara Cocoran frequently relates her success to her struggles with dyslexia, as does actor and TV/podcast host Dax Shepard, and although Steve Jobs rarely discussed it publicly, he also had dyslexia. We see a similar trend among nonfamous people, with 247 US companies reporting having at least one senior executive with a disability in 2021, according to the Disability Equality Index, which is up from 205 in 2019 (Disability:IN, 2022). Is it then possible that disability may be a source of strength for at least some?

8.1 Thriving versus Succumbing

People with disabilities, including those who are twice- or multi-exceptional, often develop in one of two ways. Some people will thrive in the face of adversity, and others will succumb to it (Bugental, 2013). So, what makes some individuals thrive in light of their disabilities, while others do not?

In some ways, the thriving versus succumbing response to adversity or disability can be reduced to a physiological response pattern to early and repeated exposure to stress-relevant hormones. According to Bugental (2013), reactions to early stressful or threatening experiences either strengthen or over-activate the body's emergency response system. Children who do not recover from early stress, such as the stress associated with a disorder, treatment of a disorder, and insensitive or abusive adults or peers in relation to a disorder, may develop a maladaptive stress response and experience physiological changes as a result of this unrelieved stress and the overactivation of the body's emergency response system. This overactivation may result in cognitive, social-emotional, and health problems, making people more likely to succumb rather than to thrive. People who thrive, however, recover from early stress and therefore experience a strengthening of the body's emergency response systems and develop an adaptive stress response, which in turn acts as a protective factor for future stressful or threatening situations. In other words, people thrive who develop healthy, adaptive resilience.

Understanding the underlying physiological stress pattern is helpful. Still, it does not address why some children recover from stress, while others do not, or why some people with specific disabilities thrive, while others do not. After all, if the mere presence of adversity or disability were sufficient to develop resilience and success, we would have a much larger group of people achieving eminence. The development of resilience in young children exposed to adversity is a complex process that depends on various individual, familial, and environmental factors, as does talent development. So, what factors contribute to the recovery or lack of recovery from early childhood stressors associated with specific disabilities? Here, we explore four possibilities: ability as a protective factor, disability as a protective factor, context as a protective factor, and the ability–disability–context interaction.

8.2 Ability as a Protective Factor

Even young children who thrive in the face of disability have been found to be adaptable to change. They tend to be good communicators, have good problem-solving skills, and have strong cognitive abilities (Masten & Barnes, 2018). So, is cognitive ability a protective factor to help them thrive?

The "masking effect" in the twice- and multi-exceptionality literature refers to the situation in which a child's exceptionalities mask one another, such that their high cognitive abilities may mask their disability, or their disability may mask their high cognitive abilities (Baum & Olenchak, 2002). This situation can be a challenge for identifying and supporting twice- and multi-exceptional children, but it is not necessarily always a bad thing. In some cases, the masking effect may benefit twice- or multi-exceptional individuals. For example, if students' high cognitive abilities enable them to compensate for their disability, they may be able to develop creative solutions to overcome their challenges. In a study conducted by Vaivre-Douret and colleagues (2020), nineteen children with Development Coordination Disorder, with an average age of nine years (and a standard deviation of 2.7 years) and having IQs between 90–110, and another nineteen comparably aged children with Developmental Coordination Disorder with IQs above 120 were compared. Development Coordination Disorder is a neurodevelopmental disorder affecting fine and gross motor skills as well as visuospatial processing, executive functioning, and attention (APA, 2013). The higher-IQ group exhibited better executive functioning and visuo-spatial constructional function when compared with the lower-IQ group. The superior executive functioning of the higher-IQ group also enabled them to apply compensatory strategies for motor coordination more effectively.

However, the masking effect can also have negative consequences if it prevents children from receiving appropriate support for, or recognition of, their strengths and challenges. For example, if students' high cognitive abilities mask their disability, they may not receive accommodations or support that could help them achieve their full potential. The same study conducted by Vaivre-Douret and colleagues (2020) found that, due to the higher-IQ group's strengths, the children concealed their disability, with the condition only becoming apparent later than for lower-IQ peers with Developmental Coordination Disorder.

Protective aspects of ability are not limited to cognitive abilities alone. Any natural ability can act as a protective factor for people with disabilities in their talent development process by providing a foundation on which they can build their skills and talents (Gagné, 2018). When individuals have natural abilities in a particular domain, they may be more likely to persist in their efforts to develop their skills, even in the face of challenges or setbacks (Gagné, 2018). For individuals with specific disabilities, natural abilities can also help to offset the challenges they may face in other areas. For example, an individual with a physical disability that limits mobility may have natural abilities in creative writing or music composition, which can provide a source of fulfillment and success that is not dependent on physical ability. In addition, pursuing natural abilities can provide a sense of identity and purpose for individuals with disabilities (Kaufman, 2013; Baum et al., 2014), who may face social stigmatization or marginalization in other areas of their lives. Developing and nurturing natural abilities can help individuals with disabilities to find a sense of belonging and accomplishment and can help to counter negative stereotypes and attitudes about disability. So, while not without limitations, ability may act as a protective factor in some ways.

8.3 Disability as a Protective Factor

If ability may be a protective factor in helping children thrive, could disability serve a similar function?

The following example is based on a true story. Two siblings, born just over a year apart, grew up in the same household and were, for the most part, given similar opportunities. The older sibling was identified as gifted in early childhood based on intelligence, and the younger sibling was identified with a neurodivergent condition in early childhood. The older sibling seemingly sailed through elementary and secondary school smoothly with occasional disruptive behavior and increasing demotivation and disengagement in the classroom but graduated early at sixteen. He attended college, where the sudden increased challenge resulted in a series of negative experiences, and he eventually dropped out. After several short-term jobs, he is now steadily employed in blue-collar work. Several years later, he still struggles with his lack of perseverance and not living up to his potential. The younger sibling struggled in elementary and secondary school due to her neurodivergent condition. The daily challenges she faced, both physically and academically, resulted in increased problem-solving skills, resilience, persistence, empathy, and compassion. All were traits that allowed her to pursue an advanced degree in human services and achieve success in a clinical profession.

This story illustrates two lessons. First, it demonstrates that analytical intelligence is often insufficient to succeed in school or beyond. Creativity, practical intelligence, wisdom, empathy, and resilience or persistence are necessary. Second, the story demonstrates that having a disability may promote the development of creativity, practical intelligence, wisdom, empathy, resilience, and persistence due to the adverse experiences associated with living in an ableist society. Presumably, this development would follow a similar process as the one explored in Section 7 on adversity. Or perhaps strengths develop in response to an adverse disability experience and are inherently part of a disability.

In recent years, researchers have increasingly explored strengths associated with various disabilities. Common strengths among people with attention deficit hyperactivity disorder (ADHD) include prosocial involvement, positive self-esteem (Brownlee et al., 2013), verbal abilities, logical thinking, reasoning (Ek et al., 2007), emotional intelligence (Climie et al., 2019), divergent thinking or creativity, adventurousness, and persistence (Holthe & Langvik, 2017; Sedgwick et al., 2019). Additionally, ADHD hyperfocus or intense focus on areas of interest could be adaptive rather than impairing (Lesch, 2018; Sedgwick et al., 2019). Similarly, individuals with dyslexia may struggle with reading, but they often exhibit enhanced spatial reasoning skills (Attree et al., 2009), curiosity (Kannangara et al., 2018), and creativity (Majeed et al., 2021). These skills can be valuable in fields such as architecture, art, and engineering. People with autism spectrum disorder (ASD) have strengths, often including attention to detail, honesty, reliability, perseverance, creativity, and a natural aptitude for programming and data analysis (Russell et al., 2019; Bury et al., 2020). Thus, these neurodiversities are associated with specific strengths that may be leveraged for talent development.

The strengths identified in individuals with disabilities arise from a combination of inherent traits and the adversity associated with the disability. For example, in the case of ASD, people may have a natural aptitude for attention to detail or certain technical skills. The challenges and difficulties associated with ASD contribute to developing problem-solving skills and perseverance. Additionally, people with neurodiversity may have inherent differences in their brain functioning that allow them to process information differently, which can lead to unique and creative solutions to problems. Therefore, the strengths of individuals with disabilities are likely a combination of inherent traits, the adversity associated with their disability, and their unique perspectives on the world. As such, disabilities may sometimes be a protective factor in talent development.

8.4 Context as a Protective Factor

Most talent development models view talent not as an innate, static ability but rather as the result of the interaction between an individual's abilities and the environment in which they develop (e.g., Gagné, 2018; Subotnik et al., 2011). As such, context plays a crucial role in the thriving versus succumbing response to having specific disabilities. Children with disabilities reared in supportive and nurturing environments are more likely to develop their talents and reach their full potential (Hauser-Cram et al., 2001). Not only do children's direct surroundings, including family, peers, and school, play important roles in the development of talents, but also the larger social, political, and economic environment, as well as cultural values, affect their talent development (Bronfenbrenner, 1979).

Societal perceptions and values of inclusion, diversity, and disabilities can significantly impact talent development, directly and indirectly. These perceptions and values can directly affect talent development by providing individuals with systemic access to support, opportunities, and resources that may otherwise be unavailable. For example, an inclusive culture may offer accommodations, such as wheelchair-accessible buildings or assistive technology, that allow individuals with specific disabilities to perform at their best. Indirectly, these cultural values can influence talent development by promoting strengths-based perceptions of and approaches to people with specific disabilities. Individuals with specific disabilities may be negatively impacted by ableist attitudes, medical models in which disabilities are seen as needing fixing, or a lack of understanding about their strengths and abilities. Conversely, an environment that values diversity and inclusion can foster a sense of belonging and promote a growth mindset, leading to greater confidence and success among people with specific disabilities.

Growing up in an environment that emphasizes the identification and nurturing of strengths and abilities rather than focusing on deficits and limitations is of crucial importance for everyone, but perhaps more so for people with specific disabilities, because how individuals view their disability is influenced by how their immediate environment and society at large view and treat their disability (Iudici et al., 2019). Positive self-perceptions and positive thoughts are central to talent development and achievement motivation (Seligman, 2011; Gentrup et al., 2020; Wigfield & Eccles, 2020). Self-perceptions influence an individual's belief in their own abilities and their confidence in tackling challenges.

Positive self-perceptions, such as believing in one's talent and potential, can foster self-efficacy – the belief that one can accomplish tasks and achieve goals (Ritchie, 2016). Self-efficacy is a powerful motivator that drives individuals to persist, invest effort, and develop their talents (Bandura, 1977). Positive self-perceptions may also contribute to resilience (Cazan & Dumitrescu, 2016). When individuals strongly believe in their abilities and see themselves as capable, they are more likely to overcome challenges and persist in their talent development. Believing in one's abilities also can result in setting more challenging goals and working diligently toward achieving those goals (Schunk, 1990). Positive self-perceptions also empower individuals with specific disabilities to advocate for their needs, interests, and opportunities. When individuals perceive themselves as talented and capable, they are more likely to assert themselves, seek resources and support, and actively participate in decision-making processes related to their talent development (Spicer, 2009). Thus, positive self-perception may be an important protective factor influenced by the context in which children grow up.

Overall, the context in which children with disabilities are reared can be a critical protective factor for their talent development. By creating supportive and nurturing environments that emphasize their strengths and provide accommodations and support for their challenges, children with disabilities are afforded the opportunity to develop and express their talents to their fullest potential.

8.5 Ability × Disability × Context = Success?

There is high variability in how people respond to physical, medical, social, and emotional challenges. Having explored the protective functions of ability, disability, and context separately, the question remains: Is having a specific disability likely to increase successful talent development, or does it promote components of successful intelligence (i.e., analytical, practical, creative, wise thinking)? And if so, why do some people thrive, while others do not? As with adversity, the simple presence of a specific disability does not guarantee success. Successful talent development among people with specific disabilities will depend, in part, on the person and how they tend to learn from their experiences and their context. Talent development is a dynamic process that occurs through interactions among individual abilities, disabilities, challenges, and environmental factors. As such, a synergetic effect may occur when students have specific abilities, disabilities, and a supportive environment that sets them up for successful talent development. So, not one of those protective factors will be the sole reason for success. The interaction is key (Bornstein, 2017).

This interaction effect can be illustrated in two distinct ways through the example of the siblings mentioned earlier in this section. The older sibling was identified as gifted, as indicated by a high level of intellectual ability. This may have initially provided an advantage in traditional educational settings, where the curriculum and pace may have aligned well with his abilities. However, intelligence alone does not guarantee success or fulfillment, and he dropped out of college. The younger sibling was identified with a neurodivergent condition, which presented unique challenges in her educational journey. These challenges resulted in the development of important skills that allowed her to achieve success in her chosen field. The contexts in which the siblings grew up, including their family environment, educational support, and societal attitudes, played significant roles in shaping their experiences and outcomes. While both siblings had similar opportunities and grew up in the same household, their individual needs and circumstances within that context – and thus the interaction among ability, disability, and context – differed. Let us examine how these factors influenced the talent development process and outcomes to demonstrate the ability–disability–context interaction.

The older sibling's early identification as gifted may have created expectations and pressures to live up to his perceived potential. He faced increasing challenges as he progressed through the education system and experienced demotivation and disengagement. The sudden increase in academic demands in college may have been overwhelming, leading to negative experiences (threat of failure, increased psychological cost, declining self-concept) and, eventually, dropout (self-handicapping). The older sibling had the cognitive ability to succeed in college but seemed to lack the psychosocial abilities, such as perseverance, motivation, and self-regulation, essential for success. These psychosocial skills may be underdeveloped for various reasons, including maladaptive beliefs around his competence (e.g., entity beliefs and high contingency of self-worth on academics) stemming from socialization or lack of adequate challenge in early education (Snyder & Linnenbrink-Garcia, 2013). His cognitive ability was a protective factor in that it got him through secondary education, and his underachievement only reached problematic levels in college. However, he was not challenged sufficiently due to a mismatch between his abilities and his environment. As such, he did not have to practice psychosocial skills such as perseverance and resilience.

It is then possible that some adversity (in place of a specific disability) may have resulted in more opportunities to practice specific psychosocial skills, as with his younger sibling. This is why some researchers have suggested that talent needs trauma (Collins et al., 2012), in that challenging experiences build the psychological strength necessary for talent development (Subotnik, 2015; Olszewski-Kubilius et al., 2019). The younger sibling's neurodivergent condition presented significant challenges throughout her educational journey. This circumstance provided a protective factor in that challenges foster the development of valuable traits such as problem-solving skills, resilience, persistence, empathy, and compassion. These qualities proved instrumental in pursuing an advanced degree and achieving success in a clinical profession in human services. However, without some natural abilities or a somewhat supportive environment, she may not have been able to bounce back from the challenges associated with her disability or not have had access to opportunities for talent development. The interaction effect also implies reciprocity between ability and disability to capture their mutual influence. Analytical, creative, practical, and wise thinking skills are both the cause and result of successful adaption to a specific disability. For example, had the younger sibling lacked the necessary cognitive ability for effective self-reflection, she may not have adapted to her challenges as well as she did to reap the rewards of that adaption.

In this scenario, interactions among ability, disability, and context influenced the talent development of each sibling in distinct ways. The older sibling's talent development trajectory was influenced by the mismatch between his abilities and contextual factors, such as adequate academic challenges in his early school career, leading to demotivation and redirection toward a different career path. By contrast, the younger sibling's talent development was shaped by her ability to navigate and overcome challenges due to her disability, leading to the acquisition of valuable skills and eventual success in her chosen field. This scenario highlights the complexity of talent development and emphasizes the importance of considering individual abilities, challenges or disabilities, and the contextual factors that influence the process.

In brief, the interaction among ability, disability, and context is crucial in determining the trajectory of talent development. To promote successful talent development, it is essential to provide individuals with the appropriate challenges, support, and opportunities for growth based on their unique combination of abilities, disabilities, and environmental factors. In doing so, we must use a strengths-based approach to identify and nurture talent among people with specific disabilities. Through understanding and harnessing the ability–disability–context interaction, we can foster the potential for talent development in individuals of all abilities and disabilities.

Conclusions

In this Element, we challenged the traditional notion of giftedness as an inherent trait. We argued for a more comprehensive understanding of giftedness. Giftedness is not a characteristic one is born with or confined within an individual, but rather emerges through the interaction among individuals, their environmental context, and the specific tasks they encounter during their developmental journey. By broadening our perspective and considering the complex interplay of individual and contextual factors, we can recognize the diverse forms of giftedness. The prevailing IQ-based paradigm of giftedness has perpetuated systemic exclusion, favoring individuals from privileged backgrounds, and neglecting the unique strengths and talents of individuals facing various challenges. It is crucial to move away from this narrow approach and embrace a strengths-based perspective that acknowledges and nurtures the potential for talent development in individuals of all abilities and disabilities, while focusing on promoting transformational and wise applications of gifts to promote a common good. By breaking free from the limitations of the IQ paradigm and embracing a more inclusive and holistic understanding of giftedness, we can foster a society where the full range of talents and strengths is recognized, valued, and developed. This Element serves as a radical rebellion against existing norms and calls for a shift toward a more equitable and empowering approach to gifted education and identification.

References

Albright, M. (2018). *Fascism: A warning*. Harper.

Alfonseca, K. (April 10, 2023). There have been more mass shootings than days in 2023, database shows. *ABC News*. https://abcnews.go.com/US/mass-shootings-days-2023-database-shows/story?id=96609874.

Ambrose, D. (2022). Morality and creativity overlapping in beneficial and harmful ways. In H. Kapoor & J. C. Kaufman (eds.), *Creativity and morality* (pp. 13–28). Elsevier.

American Psychiatric Association. (2013). *Diagnostic and statistical manual of mental disorders* (5th ed.). American Psychiatric.

Amnesty International. (October 21, 2022). Iran: At least 82 Baluchi protesters and bystanders killed in bloody crackdown. Retrieved May 2, 2023, from www.amnesty.org/en/latest/news/2022/10/iran-at-least-82-baluchi-protesters-and-bystanders-killed-in-bloody-crackdown/.

Amnesty International. (2022). Afghanistan: Human Rights Reports. Retrieved May 2, 2023, from www.amnesty.org/en/location/asia-and-the-pacific/south-asia/afghanistan/report-afghanistan/.

Ardelt, M. (2004). Wisdom as expert knowledge system: A critical review of a contemporary operationalization of an ancient concept. *Human Development, 47*, 257–285. https://doi.org/10.1159/000079154.

Atterbury, A. (April 4, 2022). DeSantis revokes Disney's special status after "Don't say gay" opposition. *Politico*. www.politico.com/news/2022/04/22/desantis-disney-special-status-dont-say-gay-00027302.

Attree, E. A., Turner, M. J., & Cowell, N. (2009). A virtual reality test identifies the visuospatial strengths of adolescents with dyslexia. *Cyber Psychology & Behavior, 12*(2), 163–168. https://doi.org/10.1089/cpb.2008.0204.

Avetisyan, A. (October 28, 2021). Russia ranked 10th in the global impunity index for the killings of journalists. *International Women's Media Foundation*. Retrieved May 2, 2023, from www.iwmf.org/2021/10/russia-ranked-10th-in-the-global-impunity-index-for-the-killings-of-journalists/.

Baltes, P. B., & Staudinger, U. M. (2000). A metaheuristic (pragmatic) to orchestrate mind and virtue toward excellence. *American Psychologist, 55*, 122–136. https://doi.org/10.1037/0003-066X.55.1.122.

Bandura, A. (1977). Self-efficacy: Toward a unifying theory of behavioral change. *Psychological Review, 84*(2), 191–215. https://doi.org/10.1037/0033-295X.84.2.191.

Bass, B. M. (1998). *Transformational leadership: Industrial, military, and educational impact*. Lawrence Erlbaum Associates.

Bass, B. M., & Riggio, R. E. (2006). *Transformational leadership: A comprehensive review of theory and research* (2nd ed.). Psychology Press.

Bass, B. M., Avolio, B. J., & Atwater, L. (1996). The transformational and transactional leadership of men and women. *Applied Psychology, 45*(1), 5–34. https://doi.org/10.1111/j.1464-0597.1996.tb00847.x.

Baum, S. M., & Olenchak, F. R. (2002). The alphabet children: GT, ADHD, and more. *Exceptionality, 10*(2), 77–91. https://doi.org/10.1207/S15327035 EX1002_3.

Baum, S. M., Schader, R. M., & Hébert, T. P. (2014). Through a different lens: Reflecting on a strengths-based, talent-focused approach for twice-exceptional learners. *Gifted Child Quarterly, 58*(4), 311–327. https://doi.org/10.1177/0016986214547632.

Beck, A. T. (1987). *Cognitive therapy of depression*. Guilford Books.

Binet, A., & Simon, T. (1905). New methods for the diagnosis of the intellectual level of subnormals. In H. H. Goddard (ed.), *Development of intelligence in children (the Binet-Simon Scale)*. Williams & Wilkins.

Binet, A., & Simon, T. (1916). *The development of intelligence in children* (E. S. Kite, trans., pp. 42–43). Williams & Wilkins.

Binet, A., Simon, T. H., & Goddard, H. H. (eds.). (1916). *The development of intelligence in children* (E. Kite, trans.). Publication of the Training School at Vineland.

Borland, J. H. (2005). Myth 2: The gifted constitute 3% to 5% of the population. Moreover, giftedness equals high IA, which is a stable measure of aptitude. *Gifted Child Quarterly, 53*(4), 236–238. https://doi.org/10.1177/0016986 209346825.

Bornstein, M. H. (2017). The specificity principle in acculturation science. *Perspectives on Psychological Science, 12*(1), 3–45. https://doi.org/10.1177/1745691616655997.

Bornstein, M. H. (2021). Creativity across the lifespan. In S. W. Russ, J. D. Hoffmann, & J. C. Kaufman (eds.). *Cambridge handbook of lifespan development of creativity* (pp. 56–97). Cambridge University Press.

Bratsberg, B., & Rogeberg, O. (2018). Flynn effect and its reversal are both environmentally caused. *Proceedings of the National Academy of Sciences, 115*(26), 6674–6678. https://doi.org/10.1073/pnas.1718793115.

Bronfenbrenner, U. (1979). *The ecology of human development: Experiments by nature and design*. Harvard University Press.

Brown, S., Brown, M., House, J., & Smith, D. (2008). Coping with spousal loss: Potential buffering effects of self-reported helping behavior. *Personality and*

Social Psychology Bulletin, *34*, 849–861. https://doi.org/10.1177/01461672 08314972.

Brownlee K., Rawana J., Franks J., et al. (2013). A systematic review of strengths and resilience outcome literature relevant to children and adolescents. *Child and Adolescent Social Work Journal*, *30*(5), 435–459. https://doi.org/10.1007/s10560-013-0301-9.

Bryant-Davis, T. (2005). Coping strategies of African American adult survivors of childhood violence. *Professional Psychology: Research and Practice*, *36* (4), 409–414. https://doi.org/10.1037/0735-7028.36.4.409.

Bugental, D. B. (2013). *Thriving in the face of childhood adversity*. Psychology Press.

Bury, S. M., Hedley, D., Uljarević, M., & Gal, E. (2020). The autism advantage at work: A critical and systematic review of current evidence. *Research in Developmental Disabilities*, *105*, 103750. https://doi.org/10.1016/j.ridd.2020 .103750.

Bushard, B. (April 3, 2023). DeSantis signs law allowing concealed guns to be carried in Florida without permits – joining 25 other states. *Forbes*. www .forbes.com/sites/brianbushard/2023/04/03/desantis-signs-law-allowing-con cealed-guns-to-be-carried-in-florida-without-permits-joining-25-other-states/?sh=5766a18f7e50.

Cazan, A. M., & Dumitrescu, S. A. (2016). Exploring the relationship between adolescent resilience, self-perception and locus of control. *Romanian Journal of Experimental Applied Psychology*, *7*(1), 283–286. https://doi.org/ 10.15303/rjeap.2016.si1.a61.

Ceci, S. J. (1996). On intelligence (expanded ed.). Harvard University Press.

Ceci, S. J. & Roazzi, A. (1994). The effects of context on cognition: Postcards from Brazil. In R. J. Sternberg & R. K. Wagner (eds.), *Mind in context: Interactionist perspectives on human intelligence* (pp. 74–101). Cambridge University Press.

Chaitin, J., & Steinberg, S. (2008). You should know better: Expressions of empathy and disregard among victims of massive social trauma. *Journal of Aggression, Maltreatment and Trauma*, *17*, 197–226. https://doi.org/ 10.1080/10926770802344851.

Chomsky, N. (1957/2015). *Syntactic structures*. Martino Fine Books.

Chowkase, A. A. (2022). Three C's conception of giftedness: A call for para-digm shift. *Gifted Education International*, *38*(3), 404–411. https://doi.org/ 10.1177/02614294211064703.

Chowkase, A. A., & Watve, S. (2021). From I to we: The three C's conception of gifted education. In R. J. Sternberg, D. Ambrose, & S. Karami (eds.),

Palgrave handbook of transformational giftedness for education (pp. 61–85). Palgrave-Macmillan.

Clayton, V. P., & Birren, J. E. (1980). The development of wisdom across the life-span: A reexamination of an ancient topic. In P. B. Baltes & O. G., Brim Jr. (eds.), *Life-span development and behavior* (Vol. 3, pp. 103–135). Academic Press.

Climie E. A., Mastoras S. M. (2015). ADHD in schools: Adopting a strengths-based perspective. *Canadian Psychology, 56*(3), 295–300. https://doi.org/10.1037/cap0000030.

Collins, D., & MacNamara, Á. (2012). The rocky road to the top: Why talent needs trauma. *Sports medicine, 42*, 907–914. https://doi.org/10.1007/BF03262302.

Condor Ferries. (2023). Plastic in the Ocean: Statistics 2020–2021. www.condorferries.co.uk/plastic-in-the-ocean-statistics.

Dabrowski, K. (1964). *Positive disintegration*. Brown.

Deary, I. J. (2020). *Intelligence: A very short introduction*. Oxford University Press.

Denchak, M. (January 11, 2023). Water pollution: Everything you need to know. *NRDC*. www.nrdc.org/stories/water-pollution-everything-you-need-know#whatis.

Disability:IN. (2022). *Disability Equality Index 2022*. www.disabilityin.org/wp-content/uploads/2022/06/DEI-Report_2022-Final.pdf.

Dittmann, M. (July 1, 2004). Standing tall pays off, study finds. *Monitor on Psychology, 35*(7). www.apa.org/monitor/julaug04/standing.

Dodge, K., Bates, J., & Pettit, G. (1990). Mechanisms in the cycle of violence. *Science, 250*, 1678–1683. https://doi.org/10.1126/science.2270481.

Dorfman, A., Moscovitch, D. A., Chopik, W. J., & Grossmann, I. (2022). None the wiser: Year-long longitudinal study on effects of adversity on wisdom. *European Journal of Personality, 36*(4), 559–575. https://doi.org/10.1177/08902070211014057.

Dörner, D. (1980). On the difficulties people have in dealing with complexity. *Simulation & Gaming, 11*(1), 87–106. https://doi.org/10.1177/104687818001100108.

Dörner, D. (1986). Diagnostik der operativen Intelligenz [Diagnosis of operative intelligence]. Diagnostica, 32(4), 290–308.

Dörner, D. (1990). The logic of failure. In D. E. Broadbent, J. T. Reason, & A. D. Baddeley (eds.), *Human factors in hazardous situations* (pp. 15–36). Clarendon Press/Oxford University Press.

Dörner, D. (1996). *The logic of failure: Recognizing and avoiding error in complex situations*. Basic Books.

Dörner, D., & Funke, J. (2017). Complex problem solving: What it is and what it is not. *Frontiers in Psychology, 8*(1153). https://doi.org/10.3389/fpsyg.2017.01153.

Drus, M., Kozbelt, A., & Hughes, R. R. (2014). Creativity, psychopathology, and emotion processing: A liberal response bias for remembering negative information is associated with higher creativity. *Creativity Research Journal, 26*(3), 251–262. https://doi.org/10.1080/10400419.2014.929400.

Eccles, J. S., & Wigfield, A. (2020). From expectancy-value theory to situated expectancy-value theory: A developmental, social cognitive, and sociocultural perspective on motivation. *Contemporary Educational Psychology, 61*, 101859. https://doi.org/10.1016/j.cedpsych.2020.101859.

Education Week. (March 27, 2023). School shootings this year: How many and where? *Education Week.* www.edweek.org/leadership/school-shootings-this-year-how-many-and-where/2023/01.

Eisenstadt, J. M. (1978). Parental loss and genius. *American Psychologist, 33*(3), 211–223. https://doi.org/10.1037/0003-066X.33.3.211.

Ek, U., Fernell, E., Westerlund, J., Holmberg, K., Olsson, P. O., & Gillberg, C. (2007). Cognitive strengths and deficits in schoolchildren with ADHD. *Acta Paediatrica, 96*(5), 756–761. https://doi.org/10.1111/j.1651-2227.2007.00297.x.

Ellis, B. J., Abrams, L. S., Masten, A. S., et al. (2020a). Hidden talents in harsh environments. *Development and Psychopathology, 1*, 1–19. https://doi.org/10.1017/S0954579420000887.

Ellis, B. J., Abrams, L. S., Masten, A. S., et al. (2020b). Hidden talents in harsh environments. *Development and Psychopathology, 34*(1), 95–113. https://doi.org/10.1017/S0954579420000887.

Ellis, B. J., Abrams, L. S., Masten, A. S., et al. (2023a). *The hidden talents model: Implications for science, policy, and practice.* Cambridge University Press.

Ellis, B. J., Abrams, L. S., Masten, A. S., et al. (2023b). *The hidden talents framework: Implications for science, policy, and practice.* Cambridge University Press.

Ericsson, K. A., & Pool, R. (2017). *Peak: Secrets from the new science of expertise.* Mariner Books.

Evangelisti, D. (2023). List of high IQ societies. *Test-Guide.* www.test-guide.com/list-high-iq-societies.html.

Feldon, D. F., Litson, K., Cahoon, B., et al. (2023). The predictive validity of the GRE across graduate outcomes: A meta-analysis of trends over time. *The Journal of Higher Education*, https://doi.org/10.1080/00221546.2023.2187177.

Ferrari, M., & Kim, J. (2019). Educating for wisdom. In R. J. Sternberg & J. Glück (eds.), *Cambridge handbook of wisdom* (pp. 347–371). Cambridge University Press.

Festinger, L., & Carlsmith, J. M. (1959). Cognitive consequences of forced compliance. *Journal of Abnormal and Social Psychology, 58*, 203–210. https://doi.org/10.1037/h0041593.

Flynn, J. R. (1987). Massive IQ gains in 14 nations. *Psychological Bulletin, 101*, 171–191. https://doi.org/10.1037/0033-2909.101.2.171.

Flynn, J. R. (2012). *Are we getting smarter?* Cambridge University Press. https://doi.org/10.1017/CBO9781139235679.

Flynn, J. R. (2016). *Does your family make you smarter? Nature, nurture, and human autonomy.* Cambridge University Press.

Flynn, J. R. (2020). Secular changes in intelligence: The "Flynn Effect." In R. J. Sternberg (ed.), *Cambridge handbook of intelligence* (2nd ed., pp. 940–963). Cambridge University Press. https://doi.org/10.1017/9781108770422.040.

Forgeard, M. J. C. (2013). Perceiving benefits after adversity: The relationship between self-reported posttraumatic growth and creativity. *Psychology of Aesthetics, Creativity, and the Arts, 7*(3), 245–264. https://doi.org/10.1037/a0031223.

Fourie, M. M., Stein, D. J., Solms, M., Gobodo-Madikizela, P., & Decety, J. (2019). Effects of early adversity and social discrimination on empathy for complex mental states: An fMRI investigation. *Scientific Reports, 9*(1), 1–14. https://doi.org/10.1038/s41598-019-49298-4.

Frankenhuis, W. E., Young, E. S., & Ellis, B. J. (2020). The hidden talents approach: Theoretical and methodological challenges. *Trends in Cognitive Sciences, 24*(7), 569–581. https://doi.org/10.1016/j.tics.2020.03.007.

Frey, M. C., & Detterman, D. K. (2004). Scholastic assessment or g? The relationship between the Scholastic Assessment Test and general cognitive ability. *Psychological Science, 15*, 373–378. https://doi.org/10.1111/j.0956-7976.2004.00687.x.

Gagné, F. (2018). Academic talent development: Theory and best practices. In S. I. Pfeiffer, E. Shaunessy-Dedrick, & M. Foley-Nicpon (eds.), *APA handbook of giftedness and talent* (pp. 163–183). American Psychological Association. https://doi.org/10.1037/0000038-011.

Gardner, H. (2011). *Frames of mind: The theory of multiple intelligences* (exp. ed.). Basic Books.

Gillen, G. (2005). Positive consequences of surviving a stroke. *American Journal of Occupational Therapy, 59*, 346–350. https://doi.org/10.1177/0146167208314972.

Gentrup, S., Lorenz, G., Kristen, C., & Kogan, I. (2020). Self-fulfilling prophecies in the classroom: Teacher expectations, teacher feedback and student achievement. *Learning and Instruction, 66*, 101296. https://doi.org/10.1016/j.learninstruc.2019.101296.

Gilman, B. J., Lovecky, D. V., Kearney, K., et al. (2013). Critical issues in the identification of gifted students with co-existing disabilities: The twice-exceptional. *SAGE Open, 3*(3). https://doi.org/10.1177/2158244013505855.

Glück, J., & Weststrate, N. (2022). The wisdom researchers and the elephant: An integrative model of wise behavior. *Personality and Social Psychology Review, 26*(4), 342–374. https://doi.org/10.1177/10888683221094650.

Gottfredson, L. S. (1997). Why g matters: The complexity of everyday life. *Intelligence, 24*(1), 79–132. https://doi.org/10.1016/S0160-2896(97)90014-3.

Grigorenko, E. L., Geissler, P. W., Prince, R., et al. (2001). The organization of Luo conceptions of intelligence: A study of implicit theories in a Kenyan village. *International Journal of Behavior Development, 25*, 367–378. https://doi.org/10.1080/01650250042000348.

Grisham, J. (2009). *The firm*. Vintage.

Grossman, F., Sorsoli, L., & Kia-Keating, M. (2006). A gale force wind: Meaning making by male survivors of childhood sexual abuse. *American Journal of Orthopsychiatry, 76*, 434–443. https://doi.org/10.1037/0002-9432.76.4.434.

Grossmann, I. Weststrate, N. M., Ardelt, M., et al. (2020). The science of wisdom in a polarized world: Knowns and unknowns. *Psychological Inquiry, 31*(2), 1–31. https://doi.org/10.1080/1047840X.2020.1750917.

Guilford, J. P. (1967). *The nature of human intelligence*. McGraw-Hill.

Guilford, J. P. (1988). Some changes in the structure-of-intellect model. *Educational and Psychological Measurement, 48*(1), 1–4. https://doi.org/10.1177/001316448804800102.

Guilford, J. P., & Hoepfner, R. (1971). *The analysis of intelligence*. McGraw-Hill.

GVI (September 28, 2022). Climate change and rising sea levels: 5 Pacific islands that no longer exist. *GVI USA*. www.gviusa.com/blog/disappearing-land-5-pacific-islands/.

Hair, N. L., Hanson, J. L., Wolfe, B. L., & Pollak, S. D. (2015). Association of child poverty, brain development, and academic achievement. *JAMA Pediatrics, 169*(9), 822–829. https://doi.org/10.1001/jamapediatrics.2015.1475.

Hardy, L., Barlow, M., Evans, L., et al. (2017). Great British medalists: Psychosocial biographies of super-elite and elite athletes from Olympic sports. *Progress in Brain Research, 232,* 1–119. https://doi.org/10.1016/bs.pbr.2017.03.004.

Hauck, G. (January 2, 2023). A record number of America's kids were injured or killed by gunfire in 2022. *USA Today.* www.usatoday.com/story/news/nation/2023/01/02/record-number-kids-shootings-2022/10956455002/.

Hauser-Cram, P., Warfield, M. E., Shonkoff, J. P., et al. (2001). Children with disabilities: A longitudinal study of child development and parent well-being. *Monographs of the society for research in child development,* (pp. 1–126). https://doi.org/10.1111/1540-5834.00151.

Hedlund, J. (2020). Practical intelligence. In R. J. Sternberg (ed.), *Cambridge handbook of intelligence* (2nd ed., pp. 736–755). Cambridge University Press.

Hegel, G. W. F. (1931). *The phenomenology of the mind* (2nd ed., J. D. Baillie, trans.). Allen & Unwin. (Original work published 1807).

Heller, K. A., Mönks, F. J., Sternberg, R. J., & Subotnik, R. F. (eds.) (2000). *International handbook of giftedness and talent.* Elsevier.

Herrnstein, R. J., & Murray, C. (1994). *The bell curve: Intelligence and class structure in American life.* Free Press.

Holthe M. E. G., & Langvik, E. (2017). The strives, struggles, and successes of women diagnosed with ADHD as adults. *SAGE Open, 7*(1), 1–12. https://doi.org/10.1177/2158244017701799.

Hook, K. (July 28, 2022). Why Russia's war in Ukraine is genocide. *Foreign Affairs.* www.foreignaffairs.com/ukraine/why-russias-war-ukraine-genocide.

Howells, K., & Fletcher, D., 2015. Sink or swim: Adversity- and growth-related experiences in Olympic swimming champions. *Psychology of Sport and Exercise, 16,* 37–48. https://doi.org/10.1016/j.psychsport.2014.08.004.

Human Rights Watch. (2021). World report 2021: North Korea. Retrieved May 2, 2023 from www.hrw.org/world-report/2021/country-chapters/north-korea.

Iudici, A., Favaretto, G., & Turchi, G. P. (2019). Community perspective: How volunteers, professionals, families and the general population construct disability: Social, clinical and health implications. *Disability and Health Journal, 12*(2), 171–179. https://doi.org/10.1016/j.dhjo.2018.11.014.

Jayawickreme, E., Brocato, N. W., & Blackie, L. E. R. (2017). Wisdom gained? Assessing relationships between adversity, personality and well-being among a late adolescent sample. *Journal of Youth Adolescence, 46,* 1179–1199. https://doi.org/10.1007/s10964-017-0648-x.

Jayawickreme, E., Infurna, F. J., Alajak, K., et al. (2021). Posttraumatic growth as positive personality change: Challenges, opportunities and recommendations. *Journal of Personality, 89*, 145–165. https://doi.org/10.1111/jopy.12591.

Jones, S. G. (November 7, 2018). The rise of far-right extremism in the United States. *Center for Strategic and International Studies.* www.csis.org/analysis/rise-far-right-extremism-united-states.

Kannangara, C. S., Carson, J., Puttaraju, S., & Allen, R. E. (2018). Not all those who wander are lost: Examining the character strengths of dyslexia. *Global Journal of Intellectual and Developmental Disabilities*, *4*(5), 555648. http://dx.doi.org/10.19080/GJIDD.2018.04.555648.

Kant, I. (1781/2008). *Critique of pure reason.* Penguin.

Karami, S., Ghahremani, M., Parra-Martinez, F. A., & Gentry, M. (2020). A polyhedron model of wisdom: A systematic review of the wisdom studies in psychology, management and leadership, and education. *Roeper Review, 42*(4), 241–257. https://doi.org/10.1080/02783193.2020.1815263.

Kaufman, A. S. (1979). *Intelligent testing with the WISC-R.* Wiley.

Kaufman, J. C., & Beghetto, R. A. (2009). Beyond big and little: The Four C Model of Creativity. *Review of General Psychology, 13*, 1–12. https://doi.org/10.1037/a0013688.

Kaufman, J. C., & Sternberg, R. J. (eds.) (2019). *Cambridge handbook of creativity* (2nd ed.). Cambridge University Press.

Kaufman, S. B. (2013). *Ungifted: Intelligence redefined.* Basic Books/Hachette Book.

King, N., Bryan, M., & Katz, L. (February 25, 2022). The real and imagined history of Ukraine. *Vox.* www.vox.com/22950915/ukraine-history-timothy-snyder-today-explained.

Koenig, K. A., Frey, M. C. & Detterman, D. K. (2008). ACT and general cognitive ability. *Intelligence, 36*, 153–160. https://doi.org/10.1016/j.intell.2007.03.005.

Kolbert, E. (April 1, 2019). Louisiana's disappearing cost. *The New Yorker.* www.newyorker.com/magazine/2019/04/01/louisianas-disappearing-coast.

Kramer, E. (1971). *Art as therapy with children.* Schocken Books.

Kuhn, T. (2012). *The structure of scientific revolutions* (50th anniversary ed.). University of Chicago Press.

Kuncel, N. R., Rose M., Ejiogu, K., & Yang, Z. (2014). Cognitive ability and socio-economic status relations with job performance. *Intelligence, 46*, 203–208. https://doi.org/10.1016/J.Intell.2014.06.003.

Lave, J. (1988). *Cognition in practice.* Cambridge University Press.

Leach-Kemon, K., & Sirull, R. (May 31, 2022). On gun violence, the United States is an outlier. *IHME*.www.healthdata.org/acting-data/gun-violence-united-states-outlier.

Lesch K. P. (2018). "Shine bright like a diamond!": Is research on high-functioning ADHD at last entering the mainstream? *Journal of Child Psychology and Psychiatry, 59*(3), 191–192. https://doi.org/10.1111/jcpp.12887.

Levitsky, D., & Ziblatt, S. (2018). *How democracies die.* Crown.

Lim, D., & DeSteno, D. (2016). Suffering and compassion: The links among adverse life experiences, empathy, compassion, and prosocial behavior. *Emotion, 16*(2), 175–182. https://doi.org/10.1037/emo0000144.

Lipman, M. (1987). Critical thinking: What can it be? *Analytic Teaching, 8*(1), 5–12.

Lipman-Blumen, J. (2006). *The allure of toxic leaders: Why we follow destructive bosses and corrupt politicians – and how we can survive them.* Oxford University Press.

Lubinski, D., & Benbow, C. P. (2006). Study of mathematically precocious youth after 35 years. *Perspectives on Psychological Science, 1*(4), 316–345, https://doi.org/10.1111/j.1745-6916.2006.00019.x.

Lubinski, D., & Benbow, C. P. (2020). Intellectual precocity: What have we learned since Terman? *Gifted Child Quarterly, 65*(1), 3–28. https://doi.org/10.1111/j.1745-6916.2006.00019.x.

Mackinstosh, E., & Elbagin, N., (April 6, 2019). Protesters gather outside Sudan's presidential compound. *CNN.* Retrieved May 2, 2023, from www.cnn.com/2019/04/06/africa/sudan-protest-presidential-compound-intl/index.html.

Majeed, N. M., Hartanto, A., & Tan, J. J. (2021). Developmental dyslexia and creativity: A meta-analysis. *Dyslexia, 27*(2), 187–203. https://doi.org/10.1002/dys.1677.

Malchiodi, C. A. (ed.). (2011). *Handbook of art therapy.* Guilford Press.

Markovits, D. (2020). *The meritocracy trap: How America's foundational myth feeds inequality, dismantles the middle class, and devours the elite.* Penguin.

Masten, A. S., & Barnes, A. J. (2018). Resilience in children: Developmental perspectives. *Children, 5*(7), 98. https://doi.org/10.3390/children5070098.

McCallum, R. S., Bell, S. M., Coles, J. T., et al. (2013). A model for screening twice-exceptional students (gifted with learning disabilities) within a response to intervention paradigm. *Gifted Child Quarterly, 57*(4), 209–222. https://doi.org/10.1177/0016986213500070.

Meichenbaum, D. (2017). *The evolution of cognitive behavior therapy: A personal and professional journey with Don Meichenbaum.* Routledge.

Miéville, C. (2010). *The city & the city.* Del Rey.

Miller, P., Votruba-Drzal, E., & Coley, R. L. (2019). Poverty and academic achievement across the urban to rural landscape: Associations with community resources and stressors. *RSF: The Russell Sage Foundation Journal of the Social Sciences*, *5*(2), 106–122. https://doi.org/10.7758/RSF.2019.5.2.06.

Mounk, Y. (2018). *The people vs. democracy: Why our freedom is in danger and how we can save it.* Harvard University Press.

Mulé, N. J. (2018). LGBTQI-identified human rights defenders: Courage in the face of adversity at the United Nations. *Gender & Development*, *26*(1), 89–101. https://doi.org/10.1080/13552074.2018.1429099.

Murray, C. (1998). *Income inequality and IQ.* AEI Press.

Neporent, L. (December 19, 2012). Stairway to heaven: Rock, pop, rap stars die young. *ABC News*. https://abcnews.go.com/Health/stairway-heaven-rock-pop-rap-stars-die-young/story?id=18018213.

Nicpon, M. F., Allmon, A., Sieck, B., & Stinson, R. D. (2011). Empirical investigation of twice-exceptionality: Where have we been and where are we going? *Gifted Child Quarterly*, *55*(1), 3–17. https://doi.org/10.1177/0016986210382575.

Nordqvist, C. (December 19, 2022). Why BMI is inaccurate and misleading. *Medical News Today*. www.medicalnewstoday.com/articles/265215.

Nuñes, T. (1994). Street intelligence. In R. J. Sternberg (ed.), Encyclopedia of human intelligence (Vol. 2, pp. 1045–1049). Macmillan.

Olszewski-Kubilius, P., & Corwith, S. (2018). Poverty, academic achievement, and giftedness: A literature review. *Gifted Child Quarterly*, *62*(1), 37–55. https://psycnet.apa.org/doi/10.1177/0016986217738015.

Olszewski-Kubilius, P., Subotnik, R. F., Davis, L. C., & Worrell, F. C. (2019). Benchmarking psychosocial skills important for talent development. *New Directions for Child and Adolescent Development*, *2019*(168), 161–176. https://doi.org/10.1002/cad.20318.

Omar, M. (2022). An Israeli–Palestinian–Jordanian confederation: Courage in the Face of Adversity. *World Affairs*, *185*(4), 724–736.

Orwell, G. (1950). *1984.* Signet.

Pals, J. L., & McAdams, D. P. (2004). The transformed self: A narrative understanding of posttraumatic growth. *Psychological Inquiry*, *15*(1), 65–69. www.jstor.org/stable/20447204.

Paulhus, D. L., & Williams, K. M. (2002). The dark triad of personality: Narcissism, Machiavellianism, and psychopathy. *Journal of Research in Personality*, *36*(6), 556–563. https://doi.org/10.1016/S0092-6566(02)00505-6.

Pfeiffer, S. (ed.) (2018). *Handbook of giftedness and gifted education: Psychoeducational theory, research, and best practices.* Springer.

Pietschnig, J., & Gittler, G. (2015). A reversal of the Flynn effect for spatial perception in German-speaking countries: Evidence from a cross-temporal IRT-based meta-analysis (1977–2014). *Intelligence, 53,* 145–153. https://doi.org/10.1016/j.intell.2015.10.004.

Plucker, J. A. (ed.). (2016). *Creativity & innovation: Theory, research, and practice.* Prufrock Press.

Plucker, J. A., Burroughs, N., & Song, R. (2010). *Mind the (other) gap! The growing excellence gap in K-12 education.* Center for Evaluation and Education Research. https://eric.ed.gov/?id=ED531840.

Plucker, J. A., Hardesty, J., & Burroughs, N. (2013). *Talent on the sidelines: Excellence gaps and America's persistent talent underclass.* Center for Education Policy Analyses.

Plucker, J. A., Makel, M. C., & Qian, M. (2019). Assessment of creativity. In J. C. Kaufman & R. J. Sternberg (eds.), *The Cambridge handbook of creativity* (2nd ed., pp. 44–68). Cambridge University Press.

Plucker, J. A., Runco, M. A., & Simonsen, M. A. (2020). Enhancement of creativity. In M. A. Runco & S. Pritzker (eds.), *Encyclopedia of creativity* (3rd ed., pp. 440–446). Elsevier.

Prince R. J., & Geissler P. W. (2001). Becoming "one who treats": A case study of a Luo healer and her grandson in western Kenya. *Educational Anthropology Quarterly, 32,* 447–471. https://doi.org/10.1525/aeq.2001.32.4.447.

Rank, O. (2004). *The myth of the birth of the hero* (expanded and updated ed.). Johns Hopkins University Press.

Reis, S. M., & Renzulli, J. S. (2009). Myth 1: The gifted and talented constitute one single homogeneous group and giftedness is a way of being that stays in the person over time and experiences. *Gifted Child Quarterly, 53*(4), 233–235. https://doi.org/10.1177/0016986209346824.

Renzulli, J. S. (1978). What makes giftedness? Reexamining a definition. *Phi Delta Kappan, 60,* 180–184. https://doi.org/10.1177/003172171109200821.

Renzulli, J. S. (2016). The three-ring conception of giftedness: A developmental model for promoting creative productivity. In S. M. Reis (ed.), *Reflections on gifted education: Critical works* (pp. 55–90). Prufrock Press.

Renzulli, J. S., & Reis, S. M. (1993). Developing creative productivity through the enrichment triad model. In S. G. Isaksen, M. C. Murdock, R. L. Firestien, & D. J. Treffinger (eds.), *Nurturing and developing creativity: The emergence of a discipline* (pp. 70–99). Ablex.

Renzulli, J. S., & Reis, S. M. (1994). Research related to the Schoolwide Enrichment Model. *Gifted Child Quarterly, 38*, 7–20. https://doi.org/10.1177/001698629403800102.

Renzulli, J. S., Koehler, J., & Fogarty, E. (2006). Operation Houndstooth intervention theory: Social capital in today's schools. *Gifted Child Today, 29*(1), 14–24. https://doi.org/10.4219/gct-2006-189.

Restore the Mississippi River Delta. (2023). Causes of Land and Loss. https://mississippiriverdelta.org/our-coastal-crisis/land-loss/.

Ritchie, L. (2016). *Fostering self-efficacy in higher education students*. Palgrave.

Ritchie, S. J., & Tucker-Drob, E. M. (2018). How much does education improve intelligence? A meta-analysis. *Psychological Science, 29*, 1358–1369. https://doi.org/10.1177/0956797618774253.

Rodríguez-Fernández, M. I., & Sternberg, R. J. (2023). Meaning in life in the gifted. *Manuscript in preparation*.

Roid, G. H. (2003). *Stanford-Binet intelligence scales, fifth edition: Technical manual*. Riverside Publishing.

Rosenthal, R., & Jacobson, L. (2003). *Pygmalion in the classroom: Expectation and pupils' intellectual development* (exp. ed.). Crown.

Runco, M. A. (1991). *Divergent thinking*. Praeger.

Runco, M. A., & Jaeger, G. J. (2012). The standard definition of creativity. *Creativity Research Journal, 24*(1), 92–96. https://doi.org/10.1080/10400419.2012.650092.

Russell, G., Kapp, S. K., Elliott, D., et al. (2019). Mapping the autistic advantage from the accounts of adults diagnosed with autism: A qualitative study. *Autism in Adulthood, 1*(2), 124–133. https://doi.org/10.1089/aut.2018.0035.

Ryan, R. M., & Deci, E. L. (2017). *Self-determination theory: Basic psychological needs in motivation, development, and wellness*. Guilford Publications.

Sackett, P. R., Kuncel, N. R., Arneson, J. J., Cooper, S. R., & Waters, S. D. (2009). Does socioeconomic status explain the relationship between admissions tests and post-secondary academic performance? *Psychological Bulletin, 135*, 1–22. https://doi.org/10.1037/a0013978.

Sackett, P. R., Shewach, O. R., & Dahlke, J. A. (2020). The predictive value of general intelligence. In R. J. Sternberg (ed.), *Human intelligence: An introduction* (pp. 381–414). Cambridge University Press.

Sandel, M. J. (2021). *The tyranny of merit: Can we find a common good?* Picador.

Santayana, G. (1905/1998). *The life of reason*. Prometheus Press.

Sarkar, M., & Fletcher, D. (2017). Adversity-related experiences are essential for Olympic success: Additional evidence and considerations. *Progress in Brain Research, 232,* 159–165. https://doi.org/10.1016/bs.pbr.2016.11.009.

Sarkar, M., Fletcher, D., Brown, D. J., (2015). What doesn't kill me ... Adversity-related experiences are vital in the development of superior Olympic performance. *Journal of Science and Medicine in Sport, 18,* 475–479. https://doi.org/10.1016/j.jsams.2014.06.010.

Schmidt, F. L., & Hunter, J. E. (1998). The validity and utility of selection methods in personnel psychology. *Psychological Bulletin, 124*(2), 262–274. https://doi.org/10.1037/0033-2909.124.2.262.

Schunk, D. H. (1990). Goal setting and self-efficacy during self-regulated learning. *Educational Psychologist, 25*(1), 71–86. https://doi.org/10.1207/s15326985ep2501_6.

Sears, R. R. (1977). Sources of life satisfactions of the Terman gifted men. *American Psychologist, 32*(2), 119–128. https://doi.org/10.1037/0003-066X.32.2.119.

Sedgwick J. A., Merwood A., & Asherson P. (2019). The positive aspects of attention deficit hyperactivity disorder: A qualitative investigation of successful adults with ADHD. *ADHD Attention Deficit and Hyperactivity Disorders, 11*(3), 241–253. https://doi.org/10.1007/s12402-018-0277-6.

Seery, M. D. (2011). Resilience: A silver lining to experiencing adverse life events? *Current Directions in Psychological Science, 20*(6), 390–394. https://doi.org/10.1177/0963721411424740.

Seligman, M. E. P. (2011). *Flourish: A visionary new understanding of happiness and well-being.* Free Press.

Simonton, D. K. (1999). Creativity from a historiometric perspective. *Handbook of Creativity, 6,* 116–133. https://doi.org/10.1016/bs.pbr.2016.11.009.

Smith, G. D., Ng, F., & Li, W. H. C. (2020). COVID-19: Emerging compassion, courage and resilience in the face of misinformation and adversity. *Journal of Clinical Nursing, 29*(9–10), 1425–1428. https://doi.org/10.1111%2Fjocn.15231.

Snyder, K. E., & Linnenbrink-Garcia, L. (2013). A developmental, person-centered approach to exploring multiple motivational pathways in gifted underachievement. *Educational Psychologist, 48*(4), 209–228. https://psycnet.apa.org/doi/10.1080/00461520.2013.835597.

Spearman, C. (1904). "General intelligence," objectively determined and measured. *The American Journal of Psychology, 15*(2), 201. https://doi.org/10.2307/1412107.

Spearman, C. (1927). *The abilities of man.* Macmillan.

Spicer, C. (2009). *The self-efficacy of gifted students*. LAP Lambert Academic Publishing.

Staudinger, U. M., & Glück, J. (2011). Psychological wisdom research: Commonalities and differences in a growing field. *Annual Review of Psychology*, *62*, 215–241. https://doi.org/10.1146/annurev.psych.121208.131659.

Stemler, S. E., Grigorenko, E. L., Jarvin, L., & Sternberg, R. J. (2006). Using the theory of successful intelligence as a basis for augmenting AP exams in psychology and statistics. *Contemporary Educational Psychology*, *31*(2), 344–376. https://doi.org/10.1016/j.cedpsych.2005.11.001.

Stemler, S., Sternberg, R. J., Grigorenko, E. L., Jarvin, L., & Sharpes, D. K. (2009). Using the theory of successful intelligence as a framework for developing assessments in AP Physics. *Contemporary Educational Psychology*, *34*, 195–209.

Sternberg, R. J. (1977). *Intelligence, information processing, and analogical reasoning: The componential analysis of human abilities*. Lawrence Erlbaum Associates.

Sternberg, R. J. (1980a). The development of linear syllogistic reasoning. *Journal of Experimental Child Psychology*, *29*, 340–356. https://doi.org/10.1016/0022-0965(80)90025-9.

Sternberg, R. J. (1980b). Representation and process in linear syllogistic reasoning. *Journal of Experimental Psychology: General*, *109*, 119–159. https://doi.org/10.1037/0096-3445.109.2.119.

Sternberg, R. J. (1981). A componential theory of intellectual giftedness. *Gifted Child Quarterly*, *25*, 86–93. https://doi.org/10.1177/001698628102500208.

Sternberg, R. J. (1985). *Beyond IQ: A triarchic theory of human intelligence*. Cambridge University Press.

Sternberg, R. J. (1993). The concept of "giftedness": A pentagonal implicit theory. *The origins and development of high ability* (pp. 5–21). CIBA Foundation.

Sternberg, R. J. (1997). *Successful intelligence*. Plume.

Sternberg, R. J. (1998a) A balance theory of wisdom. *Review of General Psychology*, *2*, 347–365. https://doi.org/10.1037/1089-2680.2.4.347.

Sternberg, R. J. (1998b). *Cupid's arrow*. Cambridge University Press.

Sternberg, R. J. (2000). Creativity is a decision. In A. L. Costa (ed.), *Teaching for intelligence II* (pp. 85–106). Skylight Training.

Sternberg, R. J. (2003a). A duplex theory of hate: Development and application to terrorism, massacres, and genocide. *Review of General Psychology*, *7*(3), 299–328. https://doi.org/10.1037/1089-2680.7.3.299.

Sternberg, R. J. (2003b). WICS as a model of giftedness. *High Ability Studies*, *14*(2), 109–137. https://doi.org/10.1080/1359813032000163807.

Sternberg, R. J. (2004). Why smart people can be so foolish. *European Psychologist*, *9*(3), 145–150. https://doi.org/10.1027/1016-9040.9.3.145.

Sternberg, R. J. (2005). Foolishness. In R. J. Sternberg & J. Jordan (eds.), *Handbook of wisdom: Psychological perspectives* (pp. 331–352). Cambridge University Press.

Sternberg, R. J. (2009). The rainbow and kaleidoscope projects: A new psychological approach to undergraduate admissions. *European Psychologist*, *14*, 279–287. https://doi.org/10.1027/1016-9040.14.4.279.

Sternberg, R. J. (2010). *College admissions for the 21st century*. Harvard University Press.

Sternberg, R. J. (2011). Slip-sliding away, down the ethical slope. *Chronicle of Higher Education*, *57*(19), A23.

Sternberg, R. J. (2016). Teaching for creativity. In R. A. Beghetto & J. C. Kaufman (eds.), *Nurturing creativity in the classroom* (2nd ed., pp. 355–380). Cambridge University Press.

Sternberg, R. J. (2017). Measuring creativity: A 40+ year retrospective. *Journal of Creative Behavior*, *53*(4), 600–609.http://dx.doi.org/10.1002/jocb.218.

Sternberg, R. J. (2018a) Creative giftedness is not just what creativity tests test: Implications of a triangular theory of creativity for understanding creative giftedness. *Roeper Review*, *40*(3), 158–165. https://doi.org/10.1080/02783193.2018.1467248.

Sternberg, R. J. (2018b). Wisdom, foolishness, and toxicity in human development. *Research in Human Development*, *15*(3–4), 200–210. https://doi.org/10.1080/15427609.2018.1491216.

Sternberg, R. J. (2019a). A theory of adaptive intelligence and its relation to general intelligence. *Journal of Intelligence*, *7*(4), 23. https://doi.org/10.3390/jintelligence7040023.

Sternberg, R. J. (2019b). Where have all the flowers of wisdom gone? An analysis of teaching of wisdom over the years. In R. J. Sternberg, H. Nusbaum, & J. Glueck (eds.) (2019). *Applying wisdom to contemporary world problems* (pp. 1–20). Palgrave-Macmillan.

Sternberg, R. J. (2019c). Why people often prefer wise guys to guys who are wise: An augmented balance theory of the production and reception of wisdom. In R. J. Sternberg & J. Glück (eds.), *Cambridge handbook of wisdom* (pp. 162–181). Cambridge University Press.

Sternberg, R. J. (2019d). Four ways to conceive of wisdom: Wisdom as a function of person, situation, person/situation interaction, or action.

Journal of Value Inquiry, 53, 479–485. https://doi.org/10.1007/s10790-019-09708-2.

Sternberg, R. J. (2020a). Cultural approaches to intelligence. In R. J. Sternberg (ed.), *Human intelligence: An introduction* (pp. 174–201). Cambridge University Press.

Sternberg, R. J. (2020b). Culture and intelligence. In *Oxford research encyclopedias, psychology*. Oxford University Press. https://doi.org/10.1093/acrefore/9780190236557.013.585.

Sternberg, R. J. (July 28, 2020c). It's time to stem malpractice in STEM admissions. *Inside Higher Ed*. www.insidehighered.com/views/2020/07/28/colleges-shouldnt-use-standardized-admissions-tests-alone-measure-scientific.

Sternberg, R. J. (2020d). Transformational giftedness. In T. L. Cross & P. Olszewski-Kubilius (eds.), *Conceptual frameworks for giftedness and talent development* (pp. 203–234). Prufrock Press.

Sternberg, R. J. (2020e). Transformational giftedness: Rethinking our paradigm for gifted education. *Roeper Review, 42*(4), 230–240. https://doi.org/10.1080/02783193.2020.1815266.

Sternberg, R. J. (2020f). The augmented theory of successful intelligence. In R. J. Sternberg (ed.), *The Cambridge handbook of intelligence* (pp. 679–708). Cambridge University Press. https://doi.org/10.1017/9781108770422.029.

Sternberg, R. J. (April 29, 2021a). Identification for utilization, not merely possession, of gifts: What matters is not gifts but rather deployment of gifts. *Gifted Education International, 28*(3), 354–361. https://doi.org/10.1177/02614294211013345.

Sternberg, R. J. (2021b). Adaptive intelligence: Intelligence is not a personal trait but rather a person x task x situation interaction. *Journal of Intelligence, 9*, 58. https://doi.org/10.3390/jintelligence9040058.

Sternberg, R. J. (2021c). *Adaptive intelligence: Surviving and thriving in a world of uncertainty*. Cambridge University Press.

Sternberg, R. J. (2021d). AWOKE: A theory of representation and process in intelligence as adaptation to the environment. *Personality and Individual Differences, 182*, 111108, https://doi.org/10.1016/j.paid.2021.111108.

Sternberg, R. J. (2021e). Transformational vs. transactional deployment of intelligence. *Journal of Intelligence, 9*(15). https://doi.org/10.3390/jintelligence9010015.

Sternberg, R. J. (2022a). The emperor has no clothes: The naked truth about the construct validity of traditional methods of gifted identification. *Roeper Review, 44*(4), 231–248.https://doi.org/10.1080/02783193.2022.2115179.

Sternberg, R. J. (2022b). The most important gift of all? The gift of courage. *Roeper Review, 44*(2), 73–81. https://doi.org/10.1080/02783193.2022.2043501.

Sternberg, R. J. (2022c). Identification for utilization, not merely possession, of gifts: What matters is not gifts but rather deployment of gifts. *Gifted Education International, 38*(3), 354–361. https://doi.org/10.1177/02614294211013345.

Sternberg, R. J. (2023a). Giftedness does not reside within a person: Defining giftedness in society is a three-step process. *Roeper Review, 45*(2), 50–60. https://doi.org/10.1080/02783193.2022.2145400.

Sternberg, R. J. (2023b). Individual, collective, and contextual aspects in the identification of giftedness. *Gifted Education International*, 1–22, https://doi.org/10.1177/02614294231156986.

Sternberg, R. J. (in press). A duplex model of giftedness. *Gifted Child Quarterly.*

Sternberg, R. J., & Ambrose, D. (eds.) (2021). *Conceptions of giftedness and talent.* Palgrave-Macmillan.

Sternberg, R. J., & Davidson, J. E. (eds.) (2005). *Conceptions of giftedness*, (2nd ed.). Cambridge University Press.

Sternberg, R. J., & Grigorenko, E. L. (1999). A smelly 113° in the shade, or, why we do field research. *APS Observer*, 12, 1, 10–11, & 20–21.

Sternberg, R. J., & Grigorenko, E. L. (eds.) (2003). *The psychology of abilities, competencies, and expertise.* Cambridge University Press.

Sternberg, R. J., & Grigorenko, E. L. (2006). Cultural intelligence and successful intelligence. *Group & Organization Management, 13* (1), 27–39.

Sternberg, R. J., & Hagen, E. S. (2019). Teaching for wisdom. In R. J. Sternberg & Glück, J. (eds.),*Cambridge handbook of wisdom* (pp. 372–406). Cambridge University Press.

Sternberg, R. J., & Hedlund, J. (2002). Practical intelligence, g, and work psychology. *Human Performance 15*(1/2), 143–160. https://doi.org/10.1207/S15327043HUP1501&02_09.

Sternberg, R. J., & Lubart, T. (2022). Beyond defiance: An augmented investment perspective on creativity. *Journal of Creative Behavior, 57*(1), 127–137. https://doi.org/10.1002/jocb.567.

Sternberg, R. J., & Lubart, T. I. (1995). *Defying the crowd: Cultivating creativity in a culture of conformity.* Free Press.

Sternberg, R. J., & Preiss, D. D. (2022). Conclusion: Intelligence does not inhere within the individual but rather in person x task x situation interactions. In R. J. Sternberg & D. D. Preiss (eds.), *Intelligence in context: The cultural and historical foundations of human intelligence* (pp. 415–431). Palgrave-Macmillan.

Sternberg, R. J. (Vol. ed.), & Reis, S. M. (Series ed.) (2004). *Definitions and conceptions of giftedness*. Corwin.

Sternberg, R. J., & Sternberg, K. (2008). *The nature of hate*. Cambridge University Press.

Sternberg, R. J., & Sternberg, K. (2017). Measuring scientific reasoning for graduate admissions in psychology and related disciplines. *Journal of Intelligence*, *5*(3), 29. https://doi.org/10.3390/jintelligence5030029.

Sternberg, R. J., & The Rainbow Project Collaborators (2006). The Rainbow Project: Enhancing the SAT through assessments of analytical, practical and creative skills. *Intelligence*, *34*(4), 321–350. https://doi.org/10.1016/j .intell.2006.01.002.

Sternberg, R. J., & Williams, W. M. (1997). Does the Graduate Record Examination predict meaningful success in the graduate training of psychologists? A case study. *American Psychologist*, *52*, 630–641. https://doi.org/ 10.1037/0003-066X.52.6.630.

Sternberg, R. J., & Zhang, L. F. (1995). What do we mean by "giftedness?" A pentagonal implicit theory. *Gifted Child Quarterly*, *39*(2), 88–94. https:// doi.org/10.1177/001698629503900205.

Sternberg, R. J., Forsythe, G. B., Hedlund, J., et al. (2000). *Practical intelligence in everyday life*. Cambridge University Press.

Sternberg, R. J., Nokes, K., Geissler, P. W., et al. (2001). The relationship between academic and practical intelligence: A case study in Kenya. *Intelligence*, *29*, 401–418. https://doi.org/10.1016/S0160-2896(01)00065-4.

Sternberg, R. J., Reznitskaya, A., & Jarvin, L. (2007). Teaching for wisdom: What matters is not just what students know, but how they use it. *The London Review of Education*, *5*(2), 143–158. https://doi.org/10.1080/ 14748460701440830.

Sternberg, R. J., Kaufman, J. C., & Grigorenko, E. L. (2008). *Applied intelligence*. Cambridge University Press.

Sternberg, R. J., Jarvin, L., & Grigorenko, E. L. (2011). *Explorations of the nature of giftedness*. Cambridge University Press.

Sternberg, R. J., Bonney, C. R., Gabora, L, & Merrifield, M. (2012). WICS: A model for college and university admissions. *Educational Psychologist*, *47* (1), 30–41. https://doi.org/10.1080/00461520.2011.638882.

Sternberg, R. J., Sternberg, K., & Todhunter, R. J. E. (2017). Measuring reasoning about teaching for graduate admissions in psychology and related disciplines. *Journal of Intelligence*, *5*(4), 34. https://doi.org/10.3390/ jintelligence5040034.

Sternberg, R. J., Wong, C. H., & Sternberg, K. (2019). The relation of tests of scientific reasoning to each other and to tests of fluid intelligence. *Journal of Intelligence, 7*(3), 20. https://doi.org/10.3390/jintelligence7030020.

Sternberg, R. J., Todhunter, R. J. E., Litvak, A., & Sternberg, R. J. (2020). The relation of scientific creativity and evaluation of scientific impact to scientific reasoning and general intelligence. *Journal of Intelligence, 8*(2), 17. https://doi.org/10.3390/jintelligence8020017.

Sternberg, R. J., Chowkase, A., Desmet, O., et al. (2021). Beyond transformational giftedness. *Education Sciences, 11*, 192. https://doi.org/10.3390/educsci11050192.

Sternberg, R. J., Ambrose, D., & Karami, S. (eds.) (2022). *Palgrave handbook of transformational giftedness for education*. Palgrave-Macmillan.

Sternberg, R. J., Tromp, C., & Karami, S. (2022). Intelligence, creativity, and wisdom are situated in the interaction among person x task x situation. In R. J. Sternberg, J. C. Kaufman, & S. Karami (eds.), *Intelligence, creativity, and wisdom: Are they really distinct?* Palgrave-Macmillan 367–386.

Subotnik, R. F. (2015). Psychosocial strength training: The missing piece in talent development. *Gifted Child Today, 38*(1), 41–48. https://doi.org/10.1177/1076217514556530.

Subotnik, R. F., Olszewski-Kubilius, P., & Worrell, F. C. (2011). Rethinking giftedness and gifted education: A proposed direction forward based on psychological science. *Psychological Science in the Public Interest, 12*, 3–54. https://doi.org/10.1177/1529100611418056.

Teasdale, T. W., & Owen, D. R. (2005). A long-term rise and recent decline in intelligence test performance: The Flynn effect in reverse. *Personality and Individual Differences, 39*(4), 837–843. https://doi.org/10.1016/j.paid.2005.01.029.

Terman, L. M. (1916). *The measurement of intelligence: An explanation of and a complete guide for the use of the Stanford revision and extension of the Binet-Simon intelligence scale*. Houghton Mifflin. https://doi.org/10.1037/10014-000.

Terman, L. M. (1925). *Mental and physical traits of a thousand gifted children: Genetic Studies of Genius, Volume 1*. Stanford University Press.

The Economist. (2002). No swots, please: We're Masai. www.economist.com/node/1048686.

Tirri, K. (2022). Educating ethical minds in gifted education. In R. J. Sternberg, D. Ambrose, & S. Karami (eds.), *Palgrave handbook of transformational giftedness for education* (pp. 387–402). Palgrave Macmillan.

TOI Staff. (March 16, 2023). Olmert calls on world leaders to shun Netanyahu for "destroying" Israel's democracy. www.timesofisrael.com/olmert-calls-on-world-leaders-to-shun-netanyahu-for-destroying-israels-democracy/.

Torrance, E. P. (1974). *Torrance Tests of Creative Thinking: Norms-Technical Manual*. Scholastic Testing Service.

Torrance, E. P. (2008). *Torrance Tests of Creative Thinking: Norms-Technical Manual*. Scholastic Testing Service.

Tromp, C., & Sternberg, R. J. (2022a). Dynamic creativity: A person x task x situation interaction framework. *Journal of Creative Behavior*, *56*(4), 553–565. http://doi.org/10.1002/jocb.551.

Tromp, C., & Sternberg, R. J. (2022b). How constraints impact creativity: An interaction paradigm. *Psychology of Aesthetics, Creativity, and the Arts*. Advance online publication. https://doi.org/10.1037/aca0000493.

University of California, Berkeley. (n.d.). *Figure 2: Excess mortality rates for major cities, 1915–1922*. Retrieved July 14, 2023, from https://u.demog .berkeley.edu/~andrew/1918/figure2.html.

Ursache, A., & Noble, K. G. (2016). Socioeconomic status, white matter, and executive function in children. *Brain and Behavior*, *6*(10): doi: 10.1002/ brb3.531.

Vaivre-Douret, L., Hamdioui, S., & Cannafarina, A. (2020). The influence of IQ levels on clinical features of developmental coordination disorder. *Journal of Psychiatry and Psychiatric Disorders*, *4*(4), 218–234. https://doi.org/ 10.26502/jppd.2572-519X0107.

Van Lith, T. (2015). Art making as a mental health recovery tool for change and coping. *Art Therapy*, *32*(1), 5–12. https://doi.org/10.1080/07421656.2015 .992826.

Vollhardt, J. R., & Staub, E. (2011). Inclusive altruism born of suffering: The relationship between adversity and prosocial attitudes and behavior toward disadvantaged outgroups. *American Journal of Orthopsychiatry*, *81*(3), 307– 315. https://doi.org/10.1111/j.1939-0025.2011.01099.x.

Walters, J., & Gardner, H. (1984). The crystallizing experience: Discovering an intellectual gift. In R. J. Sternberg & J. E. Davidson (eds.), *Conceptions of giftedness*, (pp.306–311). Cambridge University Press.

Watson, J. B. (1930). *Behaviorism* (Revised ed.). University of Chicago Press.

Weinstein, R. (2004). *Reaching higher: The power of expectations in schooling*. Harvard University Press.

Weston, A., & Imas, J. M. (2018). Creativity: Transformation of adversity. In L. Martin & N. Wilson (eds.), *The palgrave handbook of creativity at work*, (pp. 287–307). Palgrave Macmillan. https://doi.org/10.1007/978-3-319-77350-6_14.

Weststrate, N. M., & Glück, J. (2017). Hard-earned wisdom: Exploratory processing of difficult life experience is positively associated with wisdom. *Developmental Psychology, 53,* 800–814. https://doi.org/10.1037/dev0000286.

Wieder, B. (May 5, 2011). Theil fellowship pays 24 talented students $100,000 not to attend college. *The Chronicle of Higher Education.* www.chronicle.com/article/thiel-fellowship-pays-24-talented-students-100-000-not-to-attend-college/?cid2=gen_login_refresh&cid=gen_sign_in.

Wigfield, A., & Eccles, J. S. (2020). 35 years of research on students' subjective task values and motivation: A look back and a look forward. In A. J. Eliott (Ed.) *Advances in motivation science* (Vol. 7, pp. 161–198). Elsevier. https://doi.org/10.1016/bs.adms.2019.05.002.

Wittkower, M., & Wittkower, R. (2006). *Born under Saturn: The character and conduct of artists.* New York Review of Books.

Wolpe, J. (1973). *The practice of behavior therapy.* Pergamon Press.

World Health Organization (2023a). Air pollution. www.who.int/health-topics/air-pollution#tab=tab_1.

World Health Organization (2023b). HIV. www.who.int/data/gho/data/themes/hiv-aids.

Worldometer (2023a). Coronavirus death toll. www.worldometers.info/coronavirus/coronavirus-death-toll/.

Worldometer (2023b). Life expectancy of the world population. www.worldometers.info/demographics/life-expectancy/.

Ziegler, A. (2005). The actiotope model of giftedness. In R. J. Sternberg & J. E. Davidson (eds.), *Conceptions of giftedness* (2nd ed., pp. 411–437). Cambridge University Press.

Ziegler, A., & Stoeger, H. (2007). The Germanic view of giftedness. In S. N. Phillipson, & M. McCann (eds.), *Conceptions of giftedness: Sociocultural perspectives* (pp. 65–98). Routledge.

Zuckerman, H. (1983). The scientific elite: Nobel laureates' mutual influences. In R. S. Albert (ed.), *Genius and eminence: The social psychology of creativity and exceptional achievement* (Vol. 5, pp. 241–252). Pergamon.

Cambridge Elements ≡

Child Development

Marc H. Bornstein

National Institute of Child Health and Human Development, Bethesda
Institute for Fiscal Studies, London
UNICEF, New York City

Marc H. Bornstein is an Affiliate of the *Eunice Kennedy Shriver* National Institute of Child Health and Human Development, an International Research Fellow at the Institute for Fiscal Studies (London), and UNICEF Senior Advisor for Research for ECD Parenting Programmes. Bornstein is President Emeritus of the Society for Research in Child Development, Editor Emeritus of *Child Development*, and founding Editor of *Parenting: Science and Practice.*

About the Series

Child development is a lively and engaging, yet serious and real-world subject of scientific study that encompasses myriad theories, methods, substantive areas, and applied concerns. Cambridge Elements in Child Development addresses many contemporary topics in child development with unique, comprehensive, and state-of-the-art treatments of principal issues, primary currents of thinking, original perspectives, and empirical contributions to understanding early human development.

Cambridge Elements ≡

Child Development

Elements in the Series

A full series listing is available at: www.cambridge.org/EICD.